WANNABE HOOCHIE MAMA
GALLERY OF REALITIES' RED DRESS CODE

ALSO BY THYLIAS MOSS

POETRY
Hosiery Seams on a Bowlegged Woman
Pyramid of Bone
At Redbones
Rainbow Remnants in Rock Bottom Ghetto Sky
Small Congregations: New & Selected Poems
Last Chance for the Tarzan Holler
Slave Moth
Tokyo Butter

MEMOIR
Tale of a Sky-Blue Dress

FOR CHILDREN
I Want to Be

WANNABE HOOCHIE MAMA GALLERY OF REALITIES' RED DRESS CODE

NEW & SELECTED POEMS

THYLIAS MOSS

A Karen & Michael Braziller Book

PERSEA BOOKS / NEW YORK

To Higginson and my son Ansted,
and in memory of
Pamela Manual Henton (d. 4 March 2016),
like me, a Brasier.

Thanks to the editors of the following journals, in which some of these poems first appeared: *American Poetry Review, Bellingham Review, Boston Review, Callaloo, Epoch, Fiddlehead, Field, Gargoyle, Graham House Review, Indiana Review, Iowa Review, Iris, Kenyon Review, Konundrum, Michigan Quarterly Review, The Offing, Pivot, Poetry, poetryfoundation.org, Solo,* and *Sycamore Review.*

Selections from *At Redbones* are reprinted by permission of The Permissions Company on behalf of the Cleveland State University Poetry Center. All rights reserved.

Selections from *Pyramid of Bone* are reprinted by permission of the University of Virginia Press. Copyright © 1989 by the Rectors and Visitors of the University of Virginia. Reprinted by permission of the University of Virginia Press.

Persea Books, Inc.
277 Broadway
New York, NY 10007

Library of Congress Cataloging-in-Publication Data
Names: Moss, Thylias, author.
Title: Wannabe hoochie mama gallery of realities' red dress code : new & selected poems / Thylias Moss.
Description: First edition. | New York : Persea Books, [2017] | "A Karen & Michael Braziller Book."
Identifiers: LCCN 2016004329 | ISBN 9780892554751 (hardcover : alk. paper)
Classification: LCC PS3563.O8856 A6 2017 | DDC 811/.54—dc23
LC record available at http://lccn.loc.gov/2016004329

First Edition

Printed in the United States of America
Designed by Rita Lascaro

CONTENTS

from *Hosiery Seams on a Bowlegged Woman* (1983)

Alternatives for a Celibate Daughter   3
The Barren Midwife Speaks of Duty   4
Old Maids Weaving Baskets   5
St. Alexis Hospital: Visiting Hour   7
Goodness and the Salt of the Earth   8
Denial   9
Rush Hour   10
Five Miracles   11
The Day Before Kindergarten: Taluca, Alabama, 1959   13

from *Pyramid of Bone* (1989)

One for All Newborns   17
Lessons from a Mirror   18
A Reconsideration of the Blackbird   19
To Eliminate Vagueness   20
The Undertaker's Daughter Makes Bread   22
Timex Remembered   23
The Road to Todos Santos Is Closed   26
Doubts During Catastrophe   27

from *At Redbones* (1990)

Fullness   31
Lunchcounter Freedom   32
Provolone Baby   33
A Catcher for an Atomic Bouquet   34
November and Aunt Jemima   35
The Adversary   36
For Those Who Can't Peel the Potatoes Close Enough   37
Spilled Sugar   40
The Eyelid's Struggle   41
The Root of the Road   43
Hattie and the Power of Biscuits   44

Raising a Humid Flag   45

Those Men at Redbones   46

Death of the Sweet World   47

She's Florida Missouri But She Was Born in Valhermosa and Lives in Ohio   49

The Party to Which Wolves Are Invited   50

The Sin-Washing Gimmick   52

Botanical Fanaticism   53

Sunrise Comes to Second Avenue   55

A Godiva   56

from *Rainbow Remnants in Rock Bottom Ghetto Sky* (1991)

Renewal at the Pediatric Hospice   61

The Rapture of Dry Ice Burning Off Skin as the Moment of the Soul's Apotheosis   63

An Anointing   65

Tornados   67

Detour: The Death of Agnes   68

What Hung Above Our Heads Like Truce   71

The Jonah Effect   73

Special Effects   75

Interpretation of a Poem by Frost   77

The Lynching   78

The Linoleum Rhumba   80

Green Light and Gamma Ways   82

Miss Liberty Loses Pageant   85

The Warmth of Hot Chocolate   87

Congregations   89

from *Last Chance for the Tarzan Holler* (1998)

Those Who Love Bones   97

Juniper Tree of Knowledge   101

Last Chance for the Tarzan Holler   104

Ant Farm   110

Ear   113

Crystals   115

A Hot Time in a Small Town   117

Glory   119

Second Grade Art: The Stunning Chances   122

Overseeing the Cherry   124

After Reading *Beloved*   126
A Man   127
Cheating   129

from *Slave Moth* (2004)

The Tennessee Prophet Beehive Project   135

from *Tokyo Butter* (2006)

Lake Deirdre   149
The Culture of the Missing Song   152
Heads Wrapped in Flowers   157
The Culture of Saving Cindy's Face   159
Postscript Culture of Head Wraps   164
Victim of the Culture of Facelessness   166
Ghee Glee   170
The Subculture of the Wrongfully Accused   175
The Unbuttered Subculture of Cindy Birdsong   180
The Partial Mummy of Head Wrap Extension   183
Deirdre: A Search Engine *(excerpt)*   187

New Poems (2016)

Hypnosis at the Bird Factory   199
This Did Not Happen   215
Blue Coming   216
Me and Bubble Went to Memphis   218
The Glory Prelude   220
Sionon Epoch   223
Aneurism of Firmament   231
Wannabe Hoochie Mama Gallery of Realities' Red Dress Code   236
Higginson Matters in "The Magnificent Culture of Myopia"   240

Notes   246
About the Author   247

from

HOSIERY SEAMS ON

A BOWLEGGED WOMAN

(1983)

Alternatives for a Celibate Daughter

1.
This man is going to die without telling me.
It will happen while I dream of tornadoes
those frantic clouds swirling in search of mates.
I won't be caught without a man
to order my life like an alphabet:
Albert   Bernard   Clifford   Desmond   Eric   Father's
going to die but I'm afraid
to hold his hand. If I feel something
daughters shouldn't feel   I won't let go.

2.
I don't choose men wisely.
When all else failed I went to father.
Now he ignores me. He will not answer.
I shake him and he hardens into slate,
cold, smooth. What can I do?
I'm a trained daughter
yet the wreath I carry
could double as a bride's bouquet.

3.
The dream, almost a year old.
In it, his name for me is a flower: Hyacinth,
a final pink breath.

The Barren Midwife Speaks of Duty

I must get on with it. Children
aren't aware how close their mothers
come to death, as close as the sky
comes to earth at night: they touch.
The supine women aren't pretty;
how they look when it's over,
how pensile their paunches become,
like a milch cow's dewlap
and just as useless.
Second trimester bellies parade
outside my window. I want to shout:
you got that way without my help;
leave me alone. Instead
I don't even complain when the oilcloth
is stained.

I have the best job, bringing them into the world
then I'm through. Childbirth pains
foreshadow what's to come. Knowing that
I should shove the heads back,
stitch the openings.
Instead I teach these women a lesson.

Old Maids Weaving Baskets

I was with you when Valhermosa
was a river, when we held hands
to fight the current,
came ashore, couldn't let go,
huddled in the church-like
shadow of Edna's house
and weathervane. Valhermosa's
a creek now, an unjoined seam,
lovers reaching.

We met under this linden
the day Edna married her cousin,
honeymooned up north.
From her yard she could see
everything: two sets
of underwear on a limb.
You got here first, hid
behind branches, a bride
helped by veil. Bared breasts
filled your bowl of a lap.

Today's no different.
Deliberately I kept you waiting
till Edna left the window.
Despite rumors
we have those baskets,
a respectable business.
Your feet dangle, insect bites
on both ankles, while we plait
grasses, sapwood cuttings:
motions learned from breaking
blessed bread.

Later we collect berries
in the freshly made baskets,
eat from each other's hand,

tremble,
echoes fearing error.
You said a man
would leave you.

St. Alexis Hospital: Visiting Hour

I ask if she remembers
when she thought nuns never died.
I haven't seen a dead one yet,
she replies.

From under the bed she pulls out
a trunk full of rosaries.
End to end, they cover a mile.

Then off comes the heavy black skirt
and I tuck her in,
shake crumbs from her missal,
turn off the lamp, let the same
darkness touch us.

She tells me about the crazy nun
who wanted to grow wings,
that every night she massaged
her back with lilies' dew
and Mary's milk.

They can't get her temperature
down.

Goodness and the Salt of the Earth

Somebody's husband raped you while you were supposed to be in the choir pounding a tambourine, not a chest. Early Sunday morning, must have been an Easter Sunday because something came back from death, it came with a wedding ring and it was black and it smiled and it was good. You got pregnant. Good. Had an abortion. Good. That's what the Lord said in Genesis, he saw the world and what was happening, and it was still good. So you were good and turned the pages, read every line, and Lot's wife, that good woman, turned to salt because she was polite and couldn't leave without saying good-bye. You said it in the hospital: "Good-bye, baby, you never cried, just ate salt and died, just got tossed over the left shoulder. You broke. I never got a chance to see myself in you." In church the sisters shouted, fainted. O hallelujah! O the glory! Ushers came running, *smell the salt, sister; smell the salt*. Sometimes it brings you back. Sometimes it kills. Don't trust it. Stay away from bacon, ham, all cured meat. Stay away from uncles licking palms so the salt sticks. Stay away from men. Stay away from angry crowds yelling, "Salt, Peter. Salt, Peter." Ask the Saint for something else. It always rains. It always pours. Thank goodness.

Denial

This is supposed to be a denial. The Millers say I stole their toddler. The wife adds that precious wasn't even weaned. I'm supposed to say I never saw the child and that the only Millers I know is beer. I'm supposed to slap my thigh, act like a jolly lesbian who would, if she thought about stealing a toddler, give more consideration to gender. These Millers have a hyperactive boy. I'm told. I'm supposed to say I only resemble the Salvation Army general who rescues kids from abusive and burning homes. I have one of those faces that keeps turning up in newspapers, the police artist's composite sketch. I'm supposed to guffaw at irregular intervals. I'm supposed to hoist my feet on top of the desk and create a sensation by being crass and crude. On the advice of my lawyer I'm not supposed to plead insanity just demonstrate it.

The truth is I kept the baby while they vacationed. The truth is I won their child as payment for their poker debts. The truth is I'm the surrogate and I decided to keep the child. The truth is I had the child. Look at the womb print. I had the child but I lost it. The truth is I'm hooked up to this machine—lie detector, kidney dialysis, cathode ray decoder, automatic D & C and waxer, trying to get the nurse to overdose my morphine. Trying.

Rush Hour

He boards the train downtown,
same time I got on in Lee Heights.

Eastbound passes westbound.
Can't pick him out,

square-shouldered every one of them,
under 40 years old, over 40 thousand a year,

never glancing up from their papers
till they pass Quincy, Central Avenue's

gutted brownstones, record and head shops,
Joe D's Tavern where I rent the back room.

He's ashamed of what we have in common.
I just left his house. Spotless.

Five Miracles

for S.A.B., Z.N.H., L.H., C.H., M.H., et al.

1.
We were cutting corn from cobs,
separating pied kernels
into red piles, yellow, black.
We weren't told to do this.
We took it upon ourselves
to make distinctions,
showing off our mother wit:
red into bowls,
yellow into jars with dated labels,
black into the scuttle
by the stove.

2.
Lutie Watson swallowed a snake
when she drank at the creek
that lynchers sank Jo-jo's stone-filled
body in last year;
that snake must have been
his soul transformed
because now she's pregnant again,
way past the age of possibility.

3.
Went to a gypsy.
Gypsy had never seen a lifeline so long.
Stretches from my thumb to my shoulder.

4.
He may be a buck-toothed
ugly dude
but he ain't a sawed off runt.
Shoulders so broad
looks like his head
sits on a boxcar.

I go walking with him
through them I-talian sections,
them Polish and what-have-you sections,
people damn near bow.
His T-shirt (special made) says:
Home-grown in Darkest Africa.

5.
What's a *nice* colored girl like you
doing in New England?
Thinking about changing my reputation.

The Day Before Kindergarten: Taluca, Alabama, 1959

I watch daddy tear down
Mama Lelia's outhouse
with just his hands;
the snakes and slugs
didn't fret him none.
Then he takes me and mama riding.

We stop at the store,
looks like a house,
okra right in front,
chickpeas and hollyhocks.
Me and mama go in. The fan
don't move her hair.
She keeps her head down, stands
a long time at the counter.
Just wants some thread,
could get it herself,
there's a basketfull beside her.
Clerk keeps reading.

She's hurting my wrist,
I pull away, pick up a doll.
Clerk says we have to leave.
Mama grabs me and runs
right by daddy,
he's just coming in.

We hide in the car.
Mama smells like sour milk
and bleach.
Daddy comes out toting a sack,
clerk thought he was white.

When the store stars burning
I'm on Mama Lelia's porch
wanting to see

how the red
melts off peppermint.
I know it's like that.
One by one
each thing burns.
Pickle jars explode.
Mama Lelia asks me:
do it look like rain?
No'm, it don't.
Ain't God good!
She laughs.

Later,
while it's still smoking
I go poking with a stick.
Ashes look like nappy
nigger hair. Smells
like when the hot comb
gets too hot
and burns mama's neck.
This smell's so big
must have come
from a hundred necks.

Holding my doll
I look at the smoke,
could be a black man
running down the road;
then rub some ashes
on her face
cause I ain't scared
no more
of nothing.
Maybe I should be
but I ain't.

from

PYRAMID OF BONE

(1989)

One for All Newborns

They kick and flail like crabs on their backs.
Parents outside the nursery window do not believe
they might raise assassins or thieves, at the very worst
a poet or obscure jazz musician whose politics
spill loudly from his horn.
Everything about it was wonderful, the method
of conception, the gestation, the womb opening
in perfect analogy to the mind's expansion.
Then the dark succession of constricting years,
mother competing with daughter for beauty and losing,
varicose veins and hot water bottles, joy boiled away,
the arrival of knowledge that eyes are birds with clipped wings,
the sun at a 30° angle and unable to go higher, parents
who cannot push anymore, who stay by the window
looking for signs of spring
and the less familiar gait of grown progeny.
I am now at the age where I must begin to pay
for the way I treated my mother. My daughter is just like me.
The long trip home is further delayed, my presence
keeps the plane on the ground. If I get off, it will fly.
The propeller is a cross spinning like a buzz saw
about to cut through me. I am haunted and my mother is not dead.
The miracle was not birth but that I lived despite my crimes.
I treated God badly also; he is another parent
watching his kids through a window, eager to be proud
of his creation, looking for signs of spring.

Lessons from a Mirror

Snow White was nude at her wedding, she's so white
the gown seemed to disappear when she put it on.

Put me beside her and the proximity is good
for a study of chiaroscuro, not much else.

Her name aggravates me most, as if I need to be told
what's white and what isn't.

Judging strictly by appearance there's a future for me
forever at her heels, a shadow's constant worship.

Is it fair for me to live that way, unable
to get off the ground?

Turning the tables isn't fair unless they keep turning.
Then there's the danger of Russian roulette

and my disadvantage: nothing falls from the sky
to name me.

I am the empty space where the tooth was, that my tongue
rushes to fill because I can't stand vacancies.

And it's not enough. The penis just fills another
gap. And it's not enough.

When you look at me,
know that more than white is missing.

A Reconsideration of the Blackbird

Let's call him *Jim Crow*.

Let's call him *Nigger* and see if he rises
faster than when we say *abracadabra*.

Guess who's coming to dinner?
Score ten points if you said blackbird.
Score twenty points if you were more specific, as in the first line.

What do you find *from here to eternity*?
Blackbirds.

Who never sang for my father?
The blackbirds who came, one after the other, landed on the roof
and pressed it down, burying us alive.
Why didn't we jump out the windows? Didn't we have enough time?
We were outnumbered (13 on the clothesline, 4 & 20 in the pie).
We were holding hands and hugging like never before.
You could say the blackbirds did us a favor.

Let's not say that however. Instead let the crows speak.
Let them use their tongues or forfeit them.

Problem: What would we do with 13 little black tongues?

Solution: Give them away. Hold them for ransom. Make belts.
Little nooses for little necks.

Problem: The little nooses fit only fingers.

Solution: Get married.

Problem: No one's in love with the blackbirds.

Solution: Paint them white, call them visions, everyone will want one.

To Eliminate Vagueness

for Gary and the English 401 staff

Instructions: substitute irreversible damage *for* black
wherever it appears

In the red-legged locust's black raids upon midwest soybeans,
in their illicit transmission of tapeworms and parasites
to quail, turkeys, and guinea fowl,
in all the black calendar days that are supposed
to indicate the ordinary.

In operating rooms body parts black with gangrene
are excised and trash cans seem to fill with dead crows.

There's a black crust two miles thick in Soweto, some on bread,
some around eyes, most on the streets where blood dried
into its own monument.

Then my mother's black face nothing can soften, the sweating,
the forgetting to sleep, the solidarity with anyone troubling,
the compassion only I knew she felt hugging a radio, singing
spirituals, sequestering herself in her widow's bedroom
praying for women unable to pray.

And what of Europeans, what of Asians and Latins who are irreversibly
damaged, whose gangrened minds should be excised but who are not black?

One day I noticed my mother had poured her face onto mine
and had given me the spirituals and lullabies.
I sang them when baskets of black clouds dumped
their transparent flowers over the convent

and the nuns' basic black didn't get wet
and they carted the flowers home in wheelbarrows
and arranged them like lullabies
and wept silently

as we were weeping, mother and daughter together
in my father's old rocker, the damage already done.

The Undertaker's Daughter Makes Bread

Even a frigid wife yields, even a stud has a soft spot.
He's with one of them now, forgiving
any man who deserts a totally paralyzed woman.
I don't forgive him
for making me believe in resurrections.
My belief is stronger than his or he'd work in a tent
and I'd be the faith healer's daughter,
myself cured.
Dough rises for me
no matter how I treat it, how I punch it.
Loaves line the counter like closed coffins.
Something I never want
is to wake from a long sleep
hungry.

Timex Remembered

In the middle of an argument
I recall a high peak in the South Pacific,
a diver wearing only loin cloth and watch plunges,
surfaces, thrusts his watch towards the camera
and microphone; John Cameron Swazey takes over:
Timex, it takes a licking and keeps on ticking!

By fourth grade lickings were like bread crumbs,
too many to think about and irritating to the eyes.
I had seen Olivia jump from a window.
I had seen Dennis rape his sister's dolls
at her request.
I had seen a boy killed fifty yards from a hospital.
I remember telling the policeman who finally came
that the boy had dropped his bubblegum.
What would he do without the gum, without
a sweet taste forever on his tongue?
I was pushed aside. I retreated into silence, moved
through Glenville like a spirit. The pictures I took
hang even now in an internal gallery.
Morning Star Baptist Church was surely named
for something that didn't yet exist.

It didn't make sense when Tomasina's mother
whipped her up and down Durkee Avenue with a limb
from a peach tree. Tomasina had done what her mother did,
slept with a man, someone else's man.
Tomasina got a licking for her efforts,
her mother got Tomasina.
And yes, Tomasina kept on ticking,
the cross around her neck moved like a metronome
when she walked.

Then there was Blondell who stole
my piggy bank full of silver dollars
handed to my grandmother from her mother

who stole them from a white woman's pocketbook.
"She meant to pay me for services rendered," my great-grandmother said.
I said nothing when I saw Blondell again. Her gang stole forty
automobiles and dissected them. She knew no other science.
I listened to her popping Beechnut gum,
Blondell ticked like a bomb.

Louise thought her Navaho heart ticked too loudly
and I was so quiet she couldn't hear me above the racket
saying I liked her.
She returned to Piñon, Arizona in pieces
that each bore the signature of the craftsmen
who broke her with knives, bottle, and the tines
of forked tongues. *How* she said to me,
How I whispered but she didn't hear me,
she thought I said *This is how* and turned my back.
Nothing ticks between us.

The lickings haven't stopped.
Nowhere in the world have the lickings stopped.
What else translates as well as the sun
setting in a bloodbath?
Every heart bleeds just keeping us alive.
Oh the ticking, ticking. . . .
sometimes that's just Old Lady Samodale
trying to grow flowers, not even thinking
about race, not even worrying about who's winning
the human race, just doing her spring cleaning, making room
in her mind for flowers.
Rowdy youth ride by after a riot and tell her
this neighborhood is a ghetto now. They uproot her flowers
and trample them or try to smoke them.

Their Afros remind her of barbed wire.
She knows more about ghettos than they ever will.
Her daffodils were yellow as crayons.

Sometimes the ticking is Mrs. Samodale sinking
to her knees, shaking her head, going *tch, tch, tch*
a long way from Czechoslovakia. There's no freedom
anywhere, no freedom from the *Timex* watch, the accuracy
of its score.

The Road to Todos Santos Is Closed

That's a movie about events that don't happen where I live.
That's a documentary about a village you can't visit.

Remember not to ask how the black river was named
if you don't want to know what happens to blood
after the ground has been saturated.

A song comes from a rooftop pointed like a beak
and the beak is wired shut but the song gets out
and the song says the road is closed
and the song says this is not where Dorothy went
and the song says this is not what the dove saw
after the waters subsided
and the song says what *todos santos* means.

Todos santos means all that refers to God
Todos santos means all saints
Todos santos means lives of unquestionable repute
Todos santos means everything holy
        not just the seven days from Palm Sunday to Easter
        not just the magdalens and madonnas.
And the song is for those who speak English and need help
understanding exactly where it is that we can't go.

The road to Todos Santos is closed.
You can't even bribe the guards.
You can't even get them drunk to seduce them.
They are drunk. They've been seduced.
That's why they won't open the road.
Their skin is so hard you can't even shoot them.

There's an extra syllable Emilio
gives English words beginning with "s."
I wish to be as sure we'll get back what's missing.
I wish to have similar faith that Todos Santos can be accessed
without a road.

Doubts During Catastrophe

The hand of the Lord was upon me, and set me down
in the midst of the valley; it was full of bones.
                                    —*Ezekiel 37:1*

Being in God's hand doesn't mean being in a full house.
It means Mother Hubbard being a grave robber
cloaking herself in hood and cape dark as her act.
This is what one does when one has dogs to beware of:
dig up the prize begonias, a femur, fibula, a tibia, phalanges.
She didn't even love these bones when they walked the earth
in her man.

All it takes is faith
the size of a mustard seed that makes a real princess
toss and turn all night though it's under thirty mattresses.
I've never felt the wedding cake beneath my pillow,
the hard slice is now an artifact archaeologists attach
to a Jurassic Behemoth.

No better time to recall God's fascination
with his image. He put something of himself
in every creation. When he was tired
he made lazy idiots. When he had hiccups
he made tumbleweeds. When he needed a twin
he made Adam. And whenever he needed to
he watched Adam seduce Eve. And when once Eve refused
God's eyebrows raised, merged and flew off, a caracara
seeking carrion. And then there was wrath. *Vengeance*
is mine he said. And then there was his seduction
of Mary who had to submit, could not disobey the Lord.

If he told her he had not created disobedience
he lied.

Now the cyclone spirals above my house; I vow not to go to heaven
if that's the only ladder.

from

AT REDBONES

(1990)

Fullness

One day your place in line will mean the
Eucharist has run out. All because you waited
your turn. Christ's body can be cut into only
so many pieces. One day Jesus will be eaten up.
The Last Supper won't be misnamed. One day the
father will place shavings of his own blessed fingers
on your tongue and you will get back in line for
more. You will not find yourself out of line again.
The bread will rise inside you. A loaf of tongue.
Pumpernickel liver. You will be the miracle.
You will feed yourself five thousand times.

Lunchcounter Freedom

I once wanted a white man's eyes upon
me, my beauty riveting him to my slum
color. Forgetting his hands are made for my
curves, he would raise them to shield his eyes
and they would fly to my breasts with gentleness
stolen from doves.

I've made up my mind not to order a sandwich on
light bread if the waitress approaches me
with a pencil. My hat is the one I wear
the Sundays my choir doesn't sing. A dark
bird on it darkly sways to the gospel music,
trying to pull nectar from a cloth flower.
Psalms are mice in my mind, nibbling,
gnawing, tearing up my thoughts.
White men are the walls. I can't tell anyone
how badly I want water. In the mirage that
follows, the doves unfold into hammers.
They still fly to my breasts.

Because I'm nonviolent I don't act or
react. When knocked from the stool
my body takes its shape from what
it falls into. The white man cradles
his tar baby. Each magus in turn.
He fathered it, it looks just like him,
the spitting image. He can't let go of
his future. The menu offers tuna fish,
grits, beef in a sauce like desire.
He is free to choose from available
choices. An asterisk marks the special.

Provolone Baby

She threw the baby out with the bath water. He was part
of what made her dirty. In the shower she sang songs
other people had written. She uprooted the flowers on
her wallpaper. The living room looked like Swiss cheese.
She prefers provolone because she sings what others
write and the baby gets dirty all the time insider her. Dirt
originates inside. Volcanoes never spew out anything
clean just Swiss cheese, babies, lava corsages that she
won't wear because his promises were songs other
people had written about gin which she threw out
because it was bath water and she was through bathing
his forehead with isopropyl to bring him back to a time
of flowers and composition when he didn't smell like a
volcano but like a baby that never got dirty, that never
took root inside her, whose bath water she could cook in
although she wasn't a good cook, she was used to
throwing things away, the delicious going bad as if
throwing a tantrum and ruining the walls so she throws
them out, she peels her house, strips away all the dirty
layers to a provolone baby that needs a bath. *Ooh Baby,*
she sings, *ooh Baby, you make me feel so good,* she sings
because that's how the song was written, the way it's
supposed to go. The words ride suds down the drain,
shampoo blossoms melt down her back.

A Catcher for an Atomic Bouquet

I have just watched Eyes on the Prize
twenty years after the contest. I am looking
at my winnings: a husband who is not literary, a
baby from a teen-ager's body, a daughter from
a sister-in-law declared unfit.
I've had both kinds of abortions, the
voluntary, the involuntary. Stop. This
personal maze is not the prize. Stop. Writers,
my class believes, must write about what they
know, restrict themselves to expertise.
That rule leaves me no province.

I have played that game to toss a quarter
into a milk bottle with a hymen. I left the
kiosk, stuffed flamingos and Saint Bernards
still suspended from the ceiling like plucked
chickens, ducks, onions, eels at a Hangzhou
outdoor market.

When the baby tugs at me he is no prize; a prize
just doesn't force its acceptance. You could
easily look at him thinking how you didn't bring
him into the world, he isn't really your
responsibility. You just signed your name on
a sheaf of paper that could have been one of the
usual bad checks. You know, however, who's doing
all the insisting that the baby stay in the world.
Who's loving the insistence. Insistence is the prize.
The faces of Hiroshima stayed on the walls, apocalyptic
posters. No one caught the bouquet thrown at the
nuclear wedding. Exploding flowers as from a joke
shop. I've got my eyes on the flamingo withdrawing
at least one leg he insists won't be shit on.

November and Aunt Jemima

We sit at the table and that is grace,
the way one commits the prelude to kowtowing
by folding into the chair.

Usually we eat as if on a subway,
among strangers, standing to avoid the
toilet seat. Today, though, is Thanksgiving

so guilt bibs us, an extra place
is set for Aunt Jemima, the pancake box
occupies the chair, the family resemblance

unmistakable. Hips full as Southern Baptist
tents but of a different doctrine.
Teeth white as the shock of lynching, thirty-two

tombstones. Despite the headrag
neither she nor her sister that bore me
are mistaken for gypsies.

The color of corrosion, she is not called
classic. The syrup that is the liquid
version of her skin flows like the promised

milk and honey so once a year we welcome
her. Even Christ would not be welcome every
day. Especially Christ who cannot come

without judgment just as she cannot come
without pancakes, flat, humane stones
still thrown at her by those whose sins

being white are invisible as her pain, the
mix in the box after the grinding of bones.

The Adversary

I understand God's reasons for keeping
Satan to himself, the only rabbit caught
on a tiring eternal hunt. Who wouldn't want
to go a few rounds with the devil that made
one of us paint a moustache on the Virgin,
increasing the likelihood that she stay one?
Imagine having to be famous for what she never had.
She can't go a few rounds with him anyway,
being unable to afford losing all she's got,
that cat's eye virginity that has to undergo
nine immaculate lifetimes before the fad dies and
we don't care what's inside her other than transplantable
organs. We'd tear him apart if God let us.

I can't forget that God's a man, subject to
the quirks of maleness, among them that need
for adversary, for worthy opponent, for just short
of equal. And that's Satan, the runner up, the
one who almost had it all, a do-nothing second in command.
The smell of victory roses mutes his protest. The consolation
of smelling them too he takes home.

Think of it, his authority denied him by a nose, a
longer, pointier Caucasian nose. And Satan is there
for God no matter what, the original Uncle Tom.

To be the winner, God needs a run for the money, a sprinter
in the next lane with the potential to grab the gold yet
who defers, won't cross the line without more information
about the other side, without a taster, a patsy
for the poison.

For Those Who Can't Peel the Potatoes Close Enough

1.

Blondell, who engraved Bridgett's face with my nails,
looks cherubic in photos from my five-candle party.
She wasn't invited, no one thirteen was. Because she was
there in bluish skin, because she wasn't a selfish breather
she became my babysitter. Sometimes the only payment she'd
accept was three White Castle burgers.
With my eyes closed I still see her popping my buttons,
offering a choice of rapist, the knife or her younger brother.
The night before Bridgett went back to Milwaukee
Blondell bound her in the basement with the choice of heated
flat iron to kiss or either of Blondell's two sets of lips.

The point is Blondell's courtesy. Her earned position
as legend. Her thank-you when her brother turned to zip
and cry.

2.

When Jesus was thirty-three
he began his work for the kingdom,
scorpions tasted his heels,
he crossed the desert in a mirage,
walking to his death as to a
lost brother.
He always knelt on his shadow.
Now I am thirty-three
and sometimes unable to feel my right leg,
a numbness that threatened my pelvis
and my ability to feel what has been
the best part of marriage,
a numbness first felt in a restaurant,
biting through fried haddock
and my lower lip
until blood spurted and I stopped at red
as I always do.
A red carpet is a tongue of blood.

Jesus never married.
I never French kiss.

3.
My son is called Dennis
after my lawless brother-in-law
after Blondell's brother.
He completes an anti-trinity.

4.
Mrs. Arnstein doesn't know I listened
to her in the middle of the night.
With my fingers in my ears I housed
her crying in my head.
Together we watched smoke rising over
the harbor. "That's him," she said.
The Aryan woman on the Blue Bonnet box
is as excited about oleo as I would be
about ceasefire. Mrs. Arnstein needs
a rest from the past.

5.
Skylines graph rising courtesy
and are shrines to her. The story of
her sainthood is the story of the stone
at the foot of a beach, washed daily,
gleaming as with holy oil when
the water recedes
as the Red Sea did
as the flood did
skeletons in their wake.
Medusa that Blondell was, she knew better
than to look at herself so her transformation
to stone leads me to conclude the miraculous
visited. Blessed rock, holy rock, a definitive
prayer. I can put my faith in such objects.

See, I throw one
and Blondell walks on water
before she drowns.

6.
All this is to show how we
are not a godless nation. Those who can't
peel the potatoes close enough are not
doomed. Look around. Some beaten women stay
in love because Jesus stayed on the cross.
The rhythm of belts finds a refrain in church
bells. Monastic silences govern many marriages.
A jackhammer makes a pentecostal call to
worship. Tough saints like Blondell beat us
into submission, into clay God can use to
reshape us. The method of salvation doesn't
matter. Let us receive the gun's sacrament, bullets
made of petrified bits of two-thousand-year-old body
followed by the siren's benediction.

Spilled Sugar

I cannot forget the sugar on the table.
The hand that spilled it was not that of
my usual father, three layers of clothes
for a wind he felt from hallway to kitchen,
the brightest room though the lightbulbs
were greasy.

The sugar like bleached anthills of ground teeth.
It seemed to issue from open wounds in his palms.
Each day, more of Father granulated, the injury spread
like dye through cotton, staining all the wash,
condemning the house.

The gas jets on the stove shoot a blue spear
that passes my cheek like air. I stir
and the sugar dissolves, the coffee giving no evidence
that it has been sweetened and I will not taste it
to find out, my father raised to my lips, the toast burnt,
the breakfast ruined.

Neither he nor I will move from the shrine
of Mother's photo. We begin to understand
the limits of love's power. And as we do,
we have to redefine God; he is not love at all.
He is longing.

He is what he became those three days
that one third of himself was dead.

The Eyelid's Struggle

We watch the pigeons bring back
the crusts left on the curb, the stiff
contexts for rye centers. If news
were history we would still read the paper.
History tells us what is worth remembering.
Not Mother's postage-stamp sized obituary.
Grief for her would be wasted, she
did not start a war, she did not stop one.
She patted on powder two shades lighter than
her face, an inch of white lies that
rubbed off on her pillow. The lies
would not stay buried. White lies
are history, white lies are policy, broken
promises to Indians.

We need to know what happened
to the canteen that formed the base
of the lamp that vanished when
I turned it off. I couldn't find
the switch in the dark; I felt like a blind
woman choosing tomatoes and realized absence
of sight did not mean absence of prejudice.
Absence of prejudice is a white lie. Mother
wore absence of prejudice to bed, when
Father kissed her, it was on his lips.
The canteen used to hold water but we didn't thirst
in the daytime. We needed light more than water.
Overnight, though, dry dreams delivered dehydration,
soda cracker clouds cracked into Communion that
cut our tongues; that was the blood, not symbolic
wine; that was salvation, the scar tissue that
formed stops us from lying.

At my request he stopped calling me rabbit.
After that, batches of his hot slaw traveled
like lava from the kitchen. It seasoned

everything, made it taste the same.
It brought the absence of prejudice to
the palate, it burned the tastebuds, we ate
hell to eliminate it as an outcome. Above
our heads the cooing suggested immature lambs,
incomplete sacrifice. The flapping
was the eyelid's struggle with tears.
When one must learn about life from a
pigeon, one learns what hardened the crusts
in the first place. A dead rabbit
doesn't always mean new life will enter the
world, sometimes just
that something is gone, won't ever
be back, that you have killed.

The Root of the Road

My hem eats the dirt haunting
my footsteps with apparitions of flies.
The road is a tongue stretched speechless.
Where I trampled faceless, I would be this
road. Whenever possible I look for where
the mouth was, I lament its loss of hair, the
uselessness of my toes combing the dirt like
plows. My own hair hangs like old udders.
I am the milk by-pass, the shortcut to hunger.

Mistress Jane, color of dough, twisted into fancy
bread, yeasty, floury, my hands when I bathe her.
She is not the one whose rising proclaims day.
She wants the road to Natchez when she looks at me,
my back doesn't disappoint. I don't feel her hand
when it touches my shoulder to guide it. What is
on me couldn't make itself felt though I wore it all
day like an epaulet. Even after removing my calico,
her glove, a layer of air prevailed, separating our skin.

My hands circled her neck following the road's
curve. Dust flew from her mouth disguised as
breath. Had she stayed mute she would have lived,
those words *after all I've done for you* (said also
to her mirror) buried me while I held onto her.
The displaced dirt from the hastily dug grave went
on walking the parent road as me. Mistress Jane was
quite comfortable underground with other roots.
Who besides the flies will believe I held a pink flower
by its pinker stem.

Hattie and the Power of Biscuits

This one is about dignity, they all
are. Hattie was an awful big
maid. Her cannon shape was appropriate
for what came out of her. She
gave context to *Gone with the Wind*, she
is what outlived Tara in significance.

In 1939 she received her Oscar for
the best supporting role, the best job
holding up the confederacy, nourishing the
nation, the white family she was *like* a
member of without being tucked into a goose-
down bed or appearing in the albums brought out
on holidays. Hers was the power of biscuits.
What a wonder she didn't use strychnine dough.
Hers was the power of the backdoor key, the
privilege to see how they really live. What
a way to start believing in yourself, to know
you don't ever want to be white. Hattie had
her bones dyed.

Biscuits cut from her cheeks by household
pinches that today reset circuit breakers in
overloaded homes. She worked so hard
the effort churned her salty milk, babies
raised on cheesiness and butter, able to siphon
anything through a straw.

Raising a Humid Flag

Enough women over thirty are at Redbones for
the smell of Dixie Peach to translate the air.
I drink when I'm there because you must have
some transparency in this life and you can't see
through the glass till it's empty. Of course I get
next to men with broad feet and bull nostrils to
ward off isolation. You go to Redbones after
you've been everywhere else and can see the rainbow
as fraud, a colorful frown.
The best part is after midnight when the crowd
at its thickest raises a humid flag and hotcombed
hair reverts to nappy origins. I go to Redbones to
put an end to denial. Dixie Peach is a heavy pomade
like canned-ham gelatin. As it drips down foreheads
and necks, it's like tallow dripping down candles
in sacred places.

Those Men at Redbones

Those men at Redbones who call me Mama don't
want milk.

They are lucky. A drop of mine
is like a bullet. You can tell
when a boy has been raised on ammunition,
his head sprouts wire. All
those barbed afros.

Those men at Redbones who call me Mama want
to repossess.

One after the other they try
to go back where they came from.
Only the snake
has not outgrown the garden.

Death of the Sweet World

People are going to think my mother
is dead. I write about her as if she'd died
because she will. My preparation is more
necessary than morbid. She'll want me
to style her hair, touch the embalmed
cheek, slip a ring my father meant to buy
on her finger.

What will happen to the rooms
she used to clean, the wealthy widows
who asked her to iron wrinkle-free linens
and had tables set for two, coffee steaming
when she arrived? I used to tell her to get
a decent job.

Her heavy perfume scented the early morning
like olfactory fog. The bags
she carried to the bus stop made her
look homeless. She was in charge
of all the church's books except the Bible.

She didn't understand that Hungary
was a country yet knew people lived there.
When she said grace her hands swept
across the meal as if she was in love with
the broom. Now she can't eat salt or sugar,
the sweet world is gone, the sour and bitter
remain.

Life alone does not impress me. The past
is more infinite than present or future, it
enlarges each day by the amount that
the others decrease. It expands

like my understanding of my mother, those houses
were cleaner than her own, some had views

that made city lights mirror stars. Even so
she didn't mind dirt, the dust
so much like ashes of loved ones.

She's Florida Missouri But She Was
Born in Valhermosa and Lives in Ohio

My mother's named for places, not Sandusky
that has wild hair soliciting the moon like blue-black
clouds touring. Not Lorain with ways too benevolent
for lay life. Ashtabula comes closer, southern,
evangelical and accented, her feet wide as yams.

She's Florida Missouri, a railroad, sturdy boxcars
without life of their own, filled and refilled with
what no one can carry.

You just can't call somebody Ravenna who's going
to have to wash another woman's bras and panties, who's
going to wear elbow-length dishwater to formal gigs,
who's going to have to work with her hands, folding and
shuffling them in prayer.

The Party to Which Wolves Are Invited

I'm five years old.
My parents tell me I'll turn into a boy
if I kiss my elbow.
(I have a moustache because I almost
succeeded).

I like to hear them at night
trying to kiss their own elbows
and turn into each other,
she thinking to show him
what a husband should be,
he intending to teach her
a thing or two about wives.

When the moon gets full of itself
my parents do not make love.
We live in an attic. We make do.

The lightning flashes as night is executed.

I'd rather kiss toads.

Stormtrooping thunder arrives. Anne is doomed.

See Anne. See Anne run. Run, Anne, run to
Burundi, 95 of every 100 adults (and all of the
children) can't read or write or draw swastikas.

I knew it; I'm dreaming I lift violets to her nose.
She pots the scent in beer steins.

I go to summer camp in a Radio Flyer wagon.
I lift the violets to her nose. I've botched my
memory. I kiss her elbow. She's in my cabin.
She can't swim either. We kiss toads in the swamp.

The graves are muddy. The rain mistakes them for
bathtubs. The toads turn into paterollers, sell
us. From the frying pan, Anne, into the fire.
My parents do not make love. The moon is full of
itself. Look at that yellow skin; bet my bottom
dollar the baby will be mulatto. No one's on bottom,
no one's on top, my parents do not make love.
Runagate, runagate. Keep moving. Women and children
first. Every man for himself. Kiss the blood off my
elbow, please. I'm homesick. I send letters
with no return address. I don't know where I
am, where the attic is. All I know is that I smell
violets. I must be near the woods. Near wolves.
They have no elbows. I can kiss them all
day long and they won't turn into something else.

Now I want my parents to step out and yell
surprise. Otherwise, anything that moves
is a wolf.

The Sin-Washing Gimmick

Jesus' fame as a sin washer spread because
he washed sins for free. You didn't have to supply
your own soap which was useless anyway in removing
pigment. Blood sins were his
specialty. When Jesus was done, you
couldn't tell who had killed, who had been
killed. We didn't mind giving up rainbows.

My sins are white as snow now and lovely.
I didn't argue about something maybe being
whiter, Bangor, Maine, South Boston. Snow
represents white well. White is so easy to
represent. Sometimes a mirage will do.

On Father's Day, a corsage of clean sins looks
elegant on my sleeve. They petal, flake like
fully cooked haddock. I am tempted to eat them
so I know they are sins. Had Jesus eaten them
instead of being wounded by them, he would have
died anyway.

Being clean is paramount as any good mother
knows. The daily washing of underwear in case
of accident so that healing can begin with a
doctor's willing touch. Bottled Jesus is the
Clorox that whitens old sheets, makes the Klan
a brotherhood of saints.

The goal is becoming white not to stop being
sin. Not to deny identity. A diamond, for
instance, whitened coal, is ruthless in the
cutting of glass.

Botanical Fanaticism

My ancestors weren't hippies, cotton
precluded fascination with flowers.
I don't remember communes, I remember
ghettos. The riots were real, not
products of hallucinogens. Free love had
been at Redbones since black unemployment
and credit saturation.

The white women my mother cleaned
for didn't notice she had changed. I guess
it was a small event, a resurrected African
jumping out the gap in her front teeth. I
guess it looked like a cockroach; that's
what she was supposed to have, not dignity.

My mother just couldn't get excited
about the Beatles, those mops she swilled
in ammonia everyday on their heads. Besides,
she didn't work like a dog but like a woman;
they aren't the same. The hair was growing long
for the same reasons Pinocchio's nose did.

I can think only of a lesbian draping
crepe paper chains over my head to make a
black Rapunzel possible; that's how a white
woman tried to lift my burdens. At the time
I didn't reject her for being lesbian or
white but for both burdens. That was when
I didn't want Ivory soap to be what
cleaned me, made me presentable to society.
All the suds I'd seen were white, they still
are but who cares? I'm more interested in
how soap dwindles in my hand, under the faucet.

I'm old enough to remember blocks
of ice, old enough or poor enough.

I remember chipping away at it, broken
glass all over the floor. Later in the
riots, the broken glass of looting tattled
how desperate people were to keep cool.

There are roses now in my mother's yard.
Sometimes she cuts them, sets them in Pepsi
bottles throughout her rooms. She is,
I admit, being sentimental. Looting her
heart. My father who planted them is gone.
That mop in the corner
is his cane growing roots.

Sunrise Comes to Second Avenue

Daylight announces
the start of a day six hours old.

We all have thankless
jobs to do. Consider

the devotion of fishes singing
hymns without voices.

The clock's hands searching
for the lost face, a place

for the Eucharist. The man
bedded down on the roadway,

the asphalt pope out of bread,
breath and blessings.

The streetcleaner
sweeping up confessions.

A Godiva

Myself, I always thought it
a throwback revealing primate roots
I'd as soon forget. Oh but what

would I do without that stuff
softer than a hand, a spool
unwound on my head and gold
already, before

the weaver comes with that talent
I share; my one-word name
rivals the best of them:
Rumplestiltskin, God.

My calling came and I went public as
a hedge on horseback in Coventry, the
sun fermenting the color of my hair
into grog that will not

lay wasted. *Eat, drink, be merry*
those aren't nude words. I put it all
on the table for surgery, not feast.
I want to be cut through to my

black woman's heart. She had one
in 1057 as well as a continent
that had not been reconciled nor
clothed. Breasts hanging as fruit

should, unpicked sculpture on a
tree, museum pieces. She is
something good for you that is not
medicine. And I

am her transmitted, no longer
literal, needful of reasons

to take off clothes that don't explain
living, and distort everything God

gave us, while trying to be
metaphors for the gifts. If I succeed
there is a tax that will die. I ride
like a morbid Midas, my lips

and fingers coax their love objects
into the most golden silence of them all.
The usual death rider got time off
for good behavior. I just worry

that I might like this, that I'll take
my heart out of the black woman and
put it in a dead thing.

from

RAINBOW REMNANTS IN

ROCK BOTTOM GHETTO SKY

(1991)

Renewal at the Pediatric Hospice

That room that sunlight fully carpets
if you rise at dawn, they all do, seems

full of conjoined children; heads, hands, arms
uniting, at first the strength of numbers but

they are one. They learn the glory of neck
from swans and learn their dive, their song, to

float and know coupling that way, from the reflection
they plan to emancipate like legacy. Each child

is a feather, souvenir of our hoped for,
unearned, ungranted evolution.

I remember them at strange times, shopping, reaching
for instant oatmeal and coffee that spurn delay.

Then in the check-out line with carriage overflowing
I glimpse Garcia's *while-U-wait* repair sign flash

a tribute to the heart's intermittent beat. That's
the best use for the telegraph. I leave through

an automatic door in time to see them paint windows
on their fingernails, make tents with their hair,

fill the whites of their eyes with snow, sculpt
the iris into the pupil's plow that clears

the field of vision for spring in which the whites
become shells and the irises, emerging chicks.

They have X-ray visions, dwindling bone mass, access
to the snowflakes arcing under their skin

where they also wear pulmonary lace
for special, endless nights

on the town when you fall
so deeply in love

you can't get up and everyone
thinks you're dead.

The Rapture of Dry Ice Burning Off
Skin as the Moment of the Soul's Apotheosis

How will we get used to joy
if we won't hold onto it?

Not even extinction stops me; when
I've sufficient craving, I follow the buffalo,
their hair hanging below their stomachs like
fringes on Tiffany lampshades; they can be turned on
so can I by a stampede, footsteps whose sound
is my heart souped up, doctored, ninety pounds
running off a semi's invincible engine. Buffalo
heaven is Niagara Falls. There their spirit
gushes. There they still stampede and power
the generators that operate the Tiffany lamps
that let us see in some of the dark. Snow
inundates the city bearing their name; buffalo
spirit chips later melt to feed the underground,
the politically dredlocked tendrils of roots. And this
has no place in reality, is trivial juxtaposed with

the faces of addicts, their eyes practically as sunken
as extinction, gray ripples like hurdlers track lanes
under them, pupils like just more needle sites.
And their arms: flesh trying for a moon apprenticeship,
a celestial antibody. Every time I use it
the umbrella is turned inside out,
metal veins, totally hardened arteries and survival
without anything flowing within, nothing saying
life came from the sea, from anywhere but coincidence
or God's ulcer, revealed. Yet also, inside out
the umbrella tries to be a bouquet, or at least
the rugged wrapping for one that must endure much,
without dispensing coherent parcels of scent,
before the refuge of vase in a room already accustomed
to withering mind and retreating skin. But the smell
of the flowers lifts the corners of the mouth as if

the man at the center of this remorse has lifted her
in a waltz. This is as true as sickness. The Jehovah's

Witness will come to my door any minute with tracts, an
inflexible agenda and I won't let him in because
I'm painting a rosy picture with only blue and
yellow (sadness and cowardice).
I'm something of an alchemist. Extinct.
He would tell me time is running out.
I would correct him: time *ran* out; that's why
history repeats itself, why we can't advance.
What joy will come has to be here right now: Cheer
to wash the dirt away, Twenty Mule Team Borax and
Arm & Hammer to magnify Cheer's power, lemon-scented
bleach and ammonia to trick the nose, improved—changed—
Tide, almost all-purpose starch that cures any limpness
except impotence. Celebrate that there's *Master*card
to rule us, bring us to our knees, the protocol we follow
in the presence of the head of our state of ruin, the
official with us all the time, not inaccessible in
palaces or White Houses or Kremlins. Besides every
ritual is stylized, has patterns and repetitions
suitable for adaptation to dance. Here come toe shoes,
brushstrokes, oxymorons. Joy

is at our tongue tips: let the great thirsts and hungers
of the world be the *marvelous* thirsts, *glorious* hungers.
Let heartbreak be alternative to coffeebreak, five
midmorning minutes devoted to emotion.

An Anointing

Boys have to slash their fingers to become brothers. Girls trade their Kotex, me and Molly do in the mall's public facility.

Me and Molly never remember each other's birthdays. On purpose. We don't like scores of any kind. We don't wear watches or weigh ourselves.

Me and Molly have tasted beer. We drank our shampoo. We went to the doctor together and lifted our specimen cups in a toast. We didn't drink that stuff. We just gargled.

When me and Molly get the urge, we are careful to put it back exactly as we found it. It looks untouched.

Between the two of us, me and Molly have 20/20 vision.

Me and Molly are in eighth grade for good. We like it there. We adore the view. We looked both ways and decided not to cross the street. Others who'd been to the other side didn't return. It was a trap.

Me and Molly don't double date. We don't multiply anything. We don't know our multiplication tables from a coffee table. We'll never be decent waitresses, indecent ones maybe.

Me and Molly do not believe in going ape or going bananas or going Dutch. We go as who we are. We go as what we are.

Me and Molly have wiped each other's asses with ferns. Made emergency tampons of our fingers. Me and Molly made do with what we have.

Me and Molly are in love with wiping the blackboard with each other's hair. The chalk gives me and Molly an idea of what old age is like; it is dusty and makes us sneeze. We are allergic to it.

Me and Molly, that's M and M, melt in your mouth.

What are we doing in your mouth? Me and Molly bet you'll never guess. Not in a million years. We plan to be around that long. Together that long. Even if we must freeze the moment and treat the photograph like the real thing.

Me and Molly don't care what people think. We're just glad that they do.

Me and Molly lick the dew off the morning grasses but taste no honey till we lick each other's tongues.

We wear full maternity sails. We boat upon my broken water. The katabatic action begins, Molly down my canal binnacle first, her water breaking in me like an anointing.

Tornados

Truth is, I envy them
not because they dance; I out jitterbug them
as I'm shuttled through and through legs
strong as looms, weaving time. They
do black more justice than I, frenzy
of conductor of philharmonic and electricity, hair
on end, result of the charge when horns and strings release
the pent up Beethoven and Mozart. Ions played

instead of notes. The movement
is not wrath, not hormone swarm because
I saw my first forming above the church a surrogate
steeple. The morning of my first baptism and
salvation already tangible, funnel for the spirit
coming into me without losing a drop, my black
guardian angel come to rescue me before all the words

get out, *I looked over Jordan and what did I see coming for*
to carry me home. Regardez, it all comes back, even the first
grade French, when the tornado stirs up the past, bewitched spoon
lost in its own spin, like a roulette wheel that won't
be steered, like the world. They drove me underground,
tornado watches and warnings, atomic bomb drills. Adult
storms so I had to leave the room. Truth is

the tornado is a perfect nappy curl, tightly wound,
spinning wildly when I try to tamper with its nature, shunning
the hot comb and pressing oil even though if absolutely straight
I'd have the longest hair in the world. Bouffant tornadic
crown taking the royal path on a trip to town, stroll down
Tornado Alley where it intersects Memory Lane. Smoky spirit-
clouds, shadows searching for what cast them.

Detour: The Death of Agnes

The night that smelled of cigarettes,
dirty snow like piles of matted ashes.

Over my shoulder in Danbury, Connecticut
my father's thin hands wiped the rear window
and I could see more clearly behind me than
in front, the road curling back there like
possibility, future, not dead past where I

recall my father rushing readiness, me nine
months old in some kind of ersatz hiking boots
retooled from his belts; he had no intention of
ever spanking me. That Sunday, I kicked up dust

that he said was me, the flying I'd do till
I could soar. I picked up a rock that he said
was me, under my pillow that night keeping me
awake, aware, more-or-less spherical bulwark,
practically immortal, my igneous self in my hand
tasting faintly sweet, fluctuating salty. He

claimed he drove a Mercury before I was born, knew
when to stop. He once had a Studebaker dream but
couldn't smell the bakery in that so we walked
from then on, full off the smell; that was the wonder
of Wonder Bread—we didn't have to buy any; almost
got rich. Any rocks in the way were cousins come

for reunion. Cancer's not the only way to go but
is effective. Agnes' lungs were not lungs, pneumatic
flops, an old woman's flat breasts ingrown. Gestures.
Her liver was there in name only, picture of catharsis.
The year of our Lord 1980 and Calvin leaves. 1990 and
his sister Agnes. The zero years. The nothing years.
My father riding again in a Toyota, a Corolla Deluxe but
he died anyway. I hadn't meant ten years ago to

drive a hearse, my hands on the horn blessing the
blaring Isaac while the back seat patriarch, his eyes
glowing like the sky leopard's spots, went hungry
for such touching. Forgiveness

jumps in the blessed/cursed night, the hitchhiker
I didn't stop for, determined to ride. I can steer
the car to locations besides death, I learned or my
father would not taxi again with me, would have
learned from his mistake of having me save him, of
having me at all, of marrying my mother, who
ended up alone anyway, just as if he hadn't.

Isn't *Agnes* a biblical book quoted almost as often
as *Psalms?* Doctors opened her and saw no scriptures,
no prophecy, no words or mark of God; ravaged and
mangled organs: Nazi science that we couldn't go by
to identify the body. Instead, by what we felt near
it, just coming into the room, her hair short like
curtains tied way back to let in all the light that
can come in her Halsted Avenue home.

It is of course the right road, the asphalt just
the black backing of a girdling, constricting mirror
that also is a vehicle to the world of Tennessee
geese, chickens in morning feathers like the
continuation of Brasier dreams knocked only once
out of the ballpark by the same ball that
struck their brother Homer Edgar dead.

The geese honk and honk for their riders and
drivers. My grandmother before Homer's funeral
throws down grain, exact toll change, and the
chickens gather around the luck that an hour earlier
rain would have washed away

as sure as Ethel Waters knew *Darkies never dream.*
Thin hands one night pull down the moon and stars
making you detour into a field of luminous cotton
that you would call Heaven if you could.

What Hung Above Our Heads Like Truce

was also sky we think we cannot touch but
with eyes; horizons stay put like sadnesses.

What we would not even pray for
in the alcove our hands make, was

already true: *even the one-eyed mother selling mangoes*
in the street makes sure her child looks great,

the white flounce collar peeled away from her throat
like the white fish flesh filleted by cool hands whose
long finger forecast nimbus.

Cooked, the fillets seemed feathered as the dream
of a manta ray whose wings stir Atlantic salt
that dissolves as if sweet in the presence of Humpbacks
and Narwahls spraying fireworks, dolphins at the end of dives
pinning foam corsages on the waves.

There is some restitution after all.

This time when I hear them, I answer the church bells and
hear voices across the skinny phone wires and the fat snakes:

Did you call the synagogue?
Aren't you Rosenthal the butcher?

You don't realize that you don't know answers until
you hear questions.

Besides, would the collar and flounder be enough
to disprove butchery? Instead
the wrong number hears a sound too tiny for the cocking
of a gun, too sympathetic for a clock, but something
clicks, falls into place.

Be advised that we talked Xhosa, made love
as the one-eyed woman, all her mangoes in other hands,
finished a tea biscuit, stardust
falling from her lips onto flounder scales, aware
of the heaviness of all that light and that heaven
pressing, pressing down.

The Jonah Effect

Instead of mud, frisbees (plastic hubcaps) on
the ground, the fifties car was there, long
as a hearse, white as memory, Pythagorean fins

warning of sharkiness in the medium navigated,
reckless drivers changing lanes along the hypotenuse
of three-way affairs so that a majority

may rule. This was not, however, a day to retreat
into Marilyn Monroe doctrine of sarong with busty
sharkiness cutting, into the medium being navigated,

an image of woman she could not reach herself.
I was through with all that; I looked out the
window that day to see ahead, androgynous picket

fences surrounding me instead of boned corsets
and their Jonah effect. In Nineveh, as in Sodom,
the doctrine of harlots, the chorus of strumpets,

the gospel of self-seduction. The car was sent
for me, the vacant back seat where statutory rape
registers, the triangle of legs as if only geometry

is at hand. The car's nuptial paint job lies about
the condition of the bride, a bomb has been dropped
on her, as a mother she is ruined, as a nationality

she is ruined; when she looks out the window
she won't be able to find Saigon, her children
won't answer to their names but she won't be

able to call them *Rumplestiltskin,* the cure
for an archaic disease; something else
ails us, *AIDS* that sounds like cure, *emphysema*

that sounds like an Indian word for beautiful land
form, like the fifty-first state or its capital.
An automatic transmission, just sit back; cruise

control, just ride, just be a tourist in the past
because you can't change a damn thing, just live
it over and over again. White car, white whale,

white dress,
all white as a sheet,
all scared.

Special Effects

I am overwhelmed by the unprecedented
accuracy of fear.

Consider how I almost scalded it in coffee, the
spoon I mistook as a key piece of my knight's armor
sure to bring him back. How could a spoon's
full, sterling hip diminishing into leg longer,
smoother than the signature Grable gam fail?
As backup: a flock of hangers perched on the
closet rod beside the heel of my shoe and when
these meet, there is that high note of a crystal
triangle to finish what the soprano can but start;
that same metaphysical note, just an octave lower
still higher than Fay Wray's screams.
She was a spoon in Kong's hand.

Tonight's feature is *Kronos,* a
technological monster, walking mega-mousetrap,
berserk Erector set of a puberty-plagued demon.
His legs were refinery storage tanks and I
will forever understand the pistons from the way
he walked (kind of mobile trash compactor).
Grendel in armor. Knight of the electromagnetic
table. Quest of the Holy Wattage. And vegetarian,
eater strictly of power plants.

He could be made of millions of spoons
melted down and reforged.
Live by the silver spoon, die by the silver spoon
when Kronos squashes you.

When Santa was younger, thinner with dark hair
and unemployed he was probably Maynard G. Krebs,
artificial beatnik. What a scary thought.

Everything a spoon has going for it
sooner or later slides off

For instance, I am not afraid of flying but of
failing to fly.

Interpretation of a Poem by Frost

A young black girl stopped by the woods,
so young she knew only one man: Jim Crow
but she wasn't allowed to call him Mister.
The woods were his and she respected his boundaries
even in the absences of fence.
Of course she delighted in the filling up
of his woods, she so accustomed to emptiness,
to being taken at face value.
This face, her face eternally the brown
of declining autumn, watches snow inter the grass,
cling to bark making it seem indecisive
about race preference, a fast-to-melt idealism.
With the grass covered, black and white are the only options,
polarity is the only reality; corners aren't neutral
but are on edge.
She shakes off snow, defiance wasted
on the limited audience of horse.
The snow does not hypnotize her as it wants to,
as the blond sun does in making too many prefer daylight.
She has promises to keep,
the promise that she bear Jim no bastards,
the promise that she ride the horse only as long
as it is willing to accept riders,
the promise that she bear Jim no bastards,
the promise to her face that it not be mistaken as shadow,
and miles to go, more than the distance from Africa to Andover
more than the distance from black to white
before she sleeps with Jim.

The Lynching

They should have slept, would have
but had to fight the darkness, had
to build a fire and bathe a man in
flames. No

other soap's as good when
the dirt is the skin. Black since
birth, burnt by birth. His father
is not in heaven. No parent

of atrocity is in heaven. My father chokes
in the next room. It is night, darkness
has replaced air. We are white like
incandescence

yet lack light. The God in my father
does not glow. The only lamp
is the burning black man. Holy
burning, holy longing, remnants of

a genie after greed. My father
baptizes by fire same as
Jesus will. Becomes a holy ghost when
he dons his sheet, a clerical collar

out of control, Dundee Mills percale,
fifty percent cotton, dixie, confederate
and fifty percent polyester, man-made, man-
ipulated, unnatural, mulatto fiber, warp

of miscegenation.
After the bath, the man is hung as if
just his washed shirt, the parts
of him most capable of sin removed.

Charred, his flesh is bark, his body
a trunk. No sign of roots. I can't leave
him. This is limbo. This is the life after
death coming if God is an invention as were

slaves. So I spend the night, his thin moon-begot
shadow as mattress; something smouldering
keeps me warm. Patches of skin fall onto me
in places I didn't know needed mending.

The Linoleum Rhumba

On parade: some of the dancer's many personalities and
guises, the Nelson's cook, the Peabody's domestic,
the geriatric ward's bed pan handler and

her children: child of the babushka, child of
the do-rag, child of the scarf, child of the veil,
child of the wig, child of the tortilla, child of
pit, child of hominy, cornpone, and grits.

Some think she's going to shine the podium and
it's true that her bosom dusts it as she speaks:
I left Mississippi for Toledo.
I left Toledo for Watts.
Thought I would see light, but
we can't stay here, we can't live this way
all by instinct but not the instinct
bred in Toogaloo and fed Pearl water.
What my children need are commando strategies that
you'd think being who and what I am I would have.
My sour lemons are the most like grenades but
they make our mouths pucker and all we can talk about
then is brotherly love.
I've also got diamonds and spades, hearts and clubs
that I keep passing out to my young ones but Lord
if my eldest doesn't keep throwing his on the table.
I don't want him shot, so I let him shoot nothing,
not the breeze, not a family picture, not hoops.

Let me clear up a nagging misunderstanding: this
is the way to make the white woman's bed—she thinks
I make it because she is rich, she thinks I make it
to get her money, that I can't get money any other
way, no skills, no intelligence, no contribution to
society but for her four poster, but I make her bed
because on Judgment Day, you will have to sleep

in the bed you made and I make damn good ones but
she didn't make any.

Enter the cat pawing its way out of the bag and into
the cat house on Catfish Row, no story completely believed
without nasty black women, their shortchanged alphabet,
from D to W, domestic to whore, sheets binding them, their
fishnet stockings hooking innocent men trying to be disciples
or they wouldn't be studying no net.

Know what she does? Goes right on loving that man limb
by limb, the mop right out of a stick figure drawing
and something to smile about: *only the flesh is weak and*
ain't none of that on him nowhere. They're
going out tonight, a heavy date, even dancing.

Sunday found her on the mourner's bench. The song
closed in on her: *Oh, loose that man and let him go.*
Then she knew; her mop is the rib, staff of Moses, spigot
for the rock water coming then, from her clay heart, her
Mississippi mud face, tributary with Niagara destiny cutting
to the bone, leaping from chin to breast, and THUNDER so
her Lord can call her and she can answer like lightning, a
bold blaze, slap across Master's fresh face, ruddy as
the cut flowers brought in this morning to grace the altar
she'd swept clean of petals, flower crap, rose and
carnation doo doo, perfume not so much mask as sweet synonym.
She had what she needed.

She returns to the podium, kicks the cat off
the platform, speaks: *Children, ain't a damn thing to*
be sorry for this morning.

The huge crowd doesn't know what to do as
they've come resolved to apologize.

Green Light and Gamma Ways

My brother, two years in the world and
exhausted, sits, porcelain bowl on his head,
for a haircut. An all-purpose bowl, we
aren't too good to beg with it. We do
because we are good, deserving. Uncooked
rice and quarters sound the same filling it.

I am immobilized, in a red light
district. The triple XXX's on the marquis
are my parents' legal signature
and approval, my embarrassment. I hope
I don't turn red, Communist. Lichis and
tadpoles holler, the crickets tick, New
World luck, westward

expansion thanks to dynamite, Grandfather's
fingers some of the Santa Fe and Southern
Pacific lines's spikes. Crucified
by my color, sick of it, jaundiced, yellow fever,
tropical, oriental.

No one speaks this old railroad language,
the locomotive blues, no speed, no
action till a rage of steam riots. Black
fist engine through a tunnel to African
rebirth. Reroutings to the Shabazz Station
roundhouse for instructions, identity. Role
models. My nose and mouth as full as theirs,
as much potential. *Say it loud, I'm Black and
I'm proud* and there is thunder. *Say it loud,
I'm yellow and proud* and there is cheese
to stand alone, *hi-ho, the derri-o, the cheese
stands alone.*

My aunt Mei-Ting, too old for everything, has
mummy feet. Better known as lotuses, flowers,

vehicles for guilt trip, gifts for the binding
anniversary. She walks in vases. She won't
go far. Beware the trip to podiatrists.
Beware of legal fetish. Gamma ways.

My mother tells me how the boat brought her
to the arms of Miss Liberty, her new mother.
She bowed long, low. Demanded nothing, didn't claim
her rights. *I have nothing to declare.* My mother
serves, the homage of rice cakes, fish, tofu and
potatoes left on the porch for helpful,
avenging spirits. *Cats. Rats.* I say.

Miss Liberty is green, the horizon and sky
plus my yellow skin. She is a minority too.
Color of ridiculous Martian fable. And not a man.
Handicapped, disabled. Green Moslem veil.

Another immigrant. I was born
American; I know cover-up is not the answer.
Peel and strip, bump and grind, Boston's Chinatown
in the Combat Zone, as if the boys and
their war brought home. Twenty-five

cents can still buy a book, a love
manual, a first generation girl's
allowance, as long as it's English
she can learn from it, first in
her low class, *e-c-h-e-l-o-n,*
echelon ands she wins the spelling bee

while the sting operation works toward
light change, against red monopoly.
Green light is like the Pacific.
Green light is like jade.
Money changes, transforms hands, Green light

is like the power you envy. It is shined on
Miss Liberty, has no inner genesis. But it
warms her.

Miss Liberty Loses Pageant

Should be a headline but it's not
newsworthy, more ordinary than anchovies
gossiping olfactions of fishy scandal.

The Lady of the Harbor, Fatima rip-off
except she came first with a crown like
the one of the thorns on another whose cause is

masses. Avant-garde refugee from 50's horror
flick *Attack of the 50-foot Woman,* here turned
to stone fleeing Gomorrah, Gotham, some G (god-

damned) place. *There she is, Miss America, your
ideal;* there must be a mistake, Miss Liberty
should have won. Why was there a contest? And

what about that talent? Professional model, posed,
picture perfect. Mannequin displayed where the world
window shops. In case of emergency, break glass.

She lost her fire. Holds an ice-cream cone.
Maybe she'll court Prometheus, this green old
paradoxical maid in Spinster Army uniform.

Basic Training long over, revolutions too
yet she earned no stars or stripes, no rank,
not even private; she's public, communal,

free. How happy she must be, everyday
at the beach, keeping to the shallows, barely
up to her knees. No lifeguard is on duty.

Her back is to us while she changes
her mind about walking away, entering
the deep seat of meaning she thought furnished

her house. She sits at the water table,
a feast has been laid for Squanto or Hobbamock
and she is it. They will be converts. Guests

not hosts. A hot night in July, fireworks
popping instead of corn. These are new ways
of business as usual. The struggle to be taken

seriously prevails over the better instinct of
not being taken at all. She is in moonlight,
her toes loosen caviar, if the sun gets the angle

right, it will sink in her torch and proxy a candle.
How romantic is the notion. Better that she gets
the man than Dudley Do-Right whose name is plea.

The Warmth of Hot Chocolate

Somebody told me I didn't exist even though he was
looking dead at me. He said that since I defied logic,
I wasn't real for reality is one of logic's definitions.
He said I was a contradiction in terms, that one side
of me cancelled out the other side leaving nothing.
His shaking knees were like polite maracas in the small
clicking they made. His moustache seemed a misplaced
smile. My compliments did not deter him from insisting
he conversed with an empty space since there was no
such thing as an angel who doesn't believe in God.
I showed him where my wings had been recently trimmed.
Everybody thinks they grow out of the back, some people
even assume shoulder blades are all that man has left
of past glory, but my wings actually grow from my scalp,
a heavy hair that stiffens for flight by the release
of chemical secretions activated whenever I jump off a
bridge. Many angels are discovered when people trying
to commit suicide ride and tame the air. I was just
such an accident. We're simply a different species,
not intrinsically holy, just intrinsically airborne.
Demons have practical reasons for not flying; it's too
hot in their home base to endure all the hair; besides,
the heat makes the chemicals boil away so demons plummet
when they jump and keep falling. Their home base isn't
solid. Demons fall perpetually, deeper and deeper into
evil until they reach a level where even to ascend is
to fall.

I think God covets my wings. He forgot to create some
for himself when he was forging himself out of pure thoughts
rambling through the universe on the backs of neutrons.
Pure thoughts were the original cowboys. I suggested
to God that he jump off a bridge to activate the wings
he was sure to have, you never forget yourself when you
divvy up the booty, but he didn't have enough faith that
his fall wouldn't be endless. I suggested that he did

in fact create wings for himself but had forgotten; his
first godly act had been performed a long time ago, afterall.

I don't believe in him; he's just a comfortable
acquaintance, a close associate with whom I can
be myself. To believe in him would place him in
the center of the universe when he's more secure
in the fringes, that farthest corner so that he
doesn't have to look over his shoulder to nab the
backstabbers who want promotions but are tired of
waiting for him to die and set in motion the natural
evolution. God doesn't want to evolve. Has been
against evolution from its creation. He doesn't
figure many possibilities are open to him. I think
he's wise to bide his time although he pales in the
moonlight to just a glow, just the warmth of hot
chocolate spreading through the body like a subcu-
taneous halo. But to trust him implicitly would
be a mistake for he then would not have to maintain
his worthiness to be God. Even the thinnest,
flyweight modicum of doubt gives God the necessity
to prove he's worthy of the implicit trust I can
never give because I protect him from corruption,
from the complacence that rises within him sometimes,
a shadowy ever-descending brother.

Congregations

—for everybody that wanted me to get religion; I got something better.

Sunrise service and Rev. Jake is a dove, his wide
white robe that used to be our church, our tent back
when we had nothing but need of God spread like wings
and the only sermon necessary is his flight, the silk
fluttering as his preaching crescendos in a syncopated
verving of latinate reverence. White
transfigured feathers that motion blurs into one,
symbol of the trinity moving in and
out of each other like ghosts that are glare, afterglow,
memory of a fire, extinguishing tears that come
when we know we can't prolong burning.
St. Joan should still glow.
Just speaking of the glory made him faint.

Years later, his bible warms his hands, never
leaves them, a dialysis, transfusion that keeps him alive
in his retirement, behind the pulpit where he is
Pastor Dawses's shadow since Ethen Dawes as the source
of light has none, just his white bread robe shaking
crumbs like lint that hitchhike in the beams issuing
from his fingertips like Mandarin nails reminding
mostly women of sea coral, but in the light that way,
the lint, the crumbs are angel down we stuff our heads with,
pad our bras and fannies with, finish ourselves with.
Where's Jake Sardan in all this?

Waiting his turn as night vision must, trying
to be some sort of secret caravan en route to a mystic
place to verify reports of healing power, but wait
and see if that trip doesn't lead him to the same
pulpit where he window shops. A shadow, man all beard
you could say, the ominous we come to church to deny, to
be loosed from, the ominous that our perfume covers,
sweating all day in the basement kitchen, vanilla and
Creole spice (cayenne, filé powder, a wish of garlic and leek)

rubbing on the musty armpits as if to marinate.

Look around at Sis. Elden's brim wider than the arms
of the crucifix but without promises; looking
into her eyes is impossible so what could be found
there must be sought elsewhere, Tahlma Ollet's
keyboard-wide bosom always in tune (can't tell
she most died bringing a no-count into the world) unlike
the old spinet whose keys look perfect but don't deliver
the notes, the pitches. Then they come; Tahlma Ollet
shouts, from kitchen below us, the sound coming up
through water pipes and plaster, thread-bare rugs that
the patting feet beat to death, a demon killing stomp;
through our own feet whose tapping is an African
distress call probably but we're out of range, out
of touch, although you can't tell from the way Tahlma's
shout comes on up through our root system then out
of our own mouths though we're out of range of the
pepper, out of touch with the onions she peels,
holding for a moment, before the knife enters,
a globe, a honeymoon, a cook's bible that she chops
into scriptures and makes us eat, tossing them
into every course: soup, entrée, dessert.
Our shouting, our jubilation scares the ominous into
crouching behind our ribs where it intercepts what
would best serve us if it reached our hearts.

It does sometimes in the hint towards boogie-woogie
courtesy the tic in Elder Simpson's fingers, the
improvised pauses, hops, physiological product of
arthritis, spiritual product of faith, a holy rolling
of the eighty-eights when he plays *Sweet Home, 'Tis the
Old Ship of Zion*. Church starts to drift there,
crucifix, hand carved, painted brown, life-size becoming
mainstay, frame of the storefront ark serving Mt. Pleasant,
home of urban schools named for dead white presidents.

Ushers pass out bread slice shaped paper almost thick as
cardboard stapled onto tongue depressors, fans
from the House of Wills, funeral parlor, black owned
and operated—some might say death always was.
Not just grief shouts, not just fury rages.
Go, Willa, go; dance that holy dance, shake
those sinful tail feathers off! *Go on, Girl, shake*
that thing; go on, Girl, shake that thing! Let God
have his way, let the spirit take control. Luther
Migby in the balcony with the wrong ideas for saving
and the right ideas for apropos fresh ways humming
Smoky Robinson, *you really got a hold on me.* One day
he'll redirect his lust, shout and taste the fruit
of Eden, won't have to eat again till
Wednesday Prayer Meeting, Thursday Tarry Service.
Friday reserved for the wakes.

> *Presenting: The House of Wills*

Grand stucco walls, Italian villa in the slums, many
porticos, small windows—many exits for the soul that's
not supposed to be buried, not supposed to love the body
that much no matter how good a master the body's been.
Hough Avenue like a wide all-purpose arrow through the
heart, the spirit of the place. Hough Avenue like a skunk
pelt (they're pretty enough), like a gray stream through
the villa grounds, rhinestoned stream whose jewels lost
their lustre only, not identity; splendid underneath the
soot of sacrifice. *The House of Wills,* home of strength,
determination, finality, bodies dressed for their apocalyptic
meeting; nothing to do that day but get up, get moving,
get on board; that's what Elder Simpson's playing now; *there's*
a train a comin'; tilt the cross and it's a railway crossing
sign; *a train's a comin'* just like yesterday, simply
switching tracks, from underground to the sky; freedom

still the destination, hear the stationmaster call: Cleveland,
Ottawa, Heaven (that's right, *Heaven;* not New Haven anymore)—
don't get off too soon, don't slip.

No, never again into perditions, foul lovers
with the smell of a different woman on each finger, too
cheap to buy rings. I could name names but would rather
not spoil the enjoyment of Judgment.
Don't you just hate time for healing *all*
wounds? Some of the wreckage goes so far back
it's a candidate for carbon dating, select relics,
choice artifacts; I must depend, to outlaw nostalgic waxing
of the heinous, on cold facts like the Vietnam Vets black wall.
Even that cools my face when pressed against it like
a keepsake flower between the verses of Ecclesiastes.
A season for everything. A purpose. Names,
sour tastes, sweet tastes that still ache, rot
my teeth when I say them, tastes I just remember,
can't taste again, could barely swallow in the
first place; tastes that no longer satisfy, to which
my tongue is numb, immune, but still food.
Nothing can change that; still food
feeding something, substances something can live off
even if that thing shouldn't be fed. *Cause the bible
tells me so.*

Jake Sardan will probably shave his all gray head,
just ashes up there saying he's the bush extinguished,
God put out. Maybe he wouldn't burn after all, a
quick study who learns to eat fire and then learns
he can't go to heaven unless he can live off
something else, not the land either, heaven is
above that. Picture this: Jake Sardan, midway man,
running shell games at the county fair, every
once in a while belching up smoke that goes way up,
doesn't bother to come down among the sinners

except that something's wrong with this future
and with any other I can think of.

So go the other way, revert to frightening basics:
creation of the world. All this, every
damned (literally) thing there is came back from that act.
We never can know what went wrong since there was no
deviation from a moment, when all was going right,
that didn't happen.

To now need a miracle makes no sense; that's what
got us started, keeps us going. Warm *Hallelujahs,*
lush *Amens,* the sedative of the congregation's
feet tapping the floors, a soft hammering, gentle
crucifixion. Nailed to the wall there's
no denying but just for a visible means of support.
Everything's eventually good for something. It
was the time that mine was the banner offering
Sunday school class. Miss Britt
whispered to me that God was watching so
do nothing I didn't want him to see. She
didn't mean this but I thought God was
giving me audience, that I was worth watching.
Self-esteem that wouldn't quit. Ticket
out of the ghetto. Sing *how I got over!*

from

LAST CHANCE FOR THE TARZAN HOLLER

(1999)

Those Who Love Bones

1.
Wilma's hair, stringy red meat, bone fixed
vs. Scarlett's corsets, exoskeletons—

not so much bone
as dust

2.
No contest—She loved bones more (her name
won't help), common woman, common problem, didn't do anything
but love to get at the bare bones of it all, ribs, for instance,
of the ark, splendid up-turned curves, thin as digits of corpses
breaking through the crust, available for complete rescue; how she loved

them, slept once with her cheek pressing on his, trying to crush his, grind his,
next best thing to rhino horn, aphrodisiac that made Wendy fly when Peter
sprinkled it on her.

3.
Sometimes, she didn't need him
because beneath her flesh, so excessive
at all the creases it folded over like Jack-in-the-pulpit,
plant-of-peace whose arum reminds those who see it
that it's time to copulate so it's banned
from the altar, were her own

bones.   Schoolboys

bite into Jack's corm, as fleshy as a woman
of experience, and thereafter call it memory-root;
they're not likely to forget the acridity, the woman's refusal.
        There is needle-like calcium oxalate
in the root, effects of pepper on the tongue
before it burns so badly not another grace will be said

that day.

          With the burn comes *the most pure*
and white starch that bludgeoned her hands
when she set it to laundry; she nearly got to the bone.
Her customers' necks blistered from treated collars.

She loved bones, stewed neckbones slowly
so the meat would fall off, leaving liberated vertebrae
in the pan like dice (a.k.a. bones) with holes punched out;
she sucked them for hours, would not answer the phone
or rush so quickly to her feet that the rhythm of sucking
would be disrupted.   Loved to dig them up

4.
from the fat breast of capon, to contemplate the archaeology
that could happen if in the barnyard, poultry had scratched up
old teeth and swallowed them like grain; she hadn't yet found
canines or incisors in the carcass on her plate, white napkin
across her lap as if it was time for gynecology, but remained dedicated
to blackened, rounded bones from thighs, legs, the ends
just like knuckles tapped for sweetness when she sucked
making up for what didn't happen when she was born.
She loved bones best
                    when they were cleaned, varnished, dried,
a complete skeleton of a flounder displayed like a harp.
She loved the skeleton of Joseph Merrick but not as much
as the bony pop star who reportedly wanted to purchase it
for a million dollars from a museum of human remains
at the Royal London College of Medicine. Merrick's bones
had been boiled once already
so they could be mounted. Proteus syndrome,
some say; the pop star
has another.

She loved bones so much she vigorously rubbed wrinkle cream
into her face so she could feel her cheekbones, but this did nothing
for progesterone and estrogen's monthly crop of white-heads, white spots
like those that killed all the pimelodellas in the fish tank; or could be eczema,
ordinary papules, but given the wasting

syndrome she volunteers to see, hospice 1996, soon the bones
will be on the table
and they will tell everything; they're such suckers
for forensic medicine.
                           Even after long silences   they may be exhumed
and even if the surviving fragment is just a piece of skullcap
no bigger than a nicotine patch, William Maples

still can tell how alligators gnawed it at the bottom
of a river two years after the hatchet man put it there; there's
a bible of bones   in a barn in the former Yugoslavia

5.
and thick as grief around Pol Pot's feet. Pray for these anchors,
pray for *the hamfat man's* lowered minstrel standard
to celebrate the awkwardness of problem bones   on Merrick's right
side as if his share of   a black mama's unlimited access to blight,
her compulsory burden to oppose the elegant left(over)'s
classic countenance; he got a good sinistrous limb (pity not a good foot)
from that miscegenetic split personality, rapture of Canaan seceding
from the cedars of Lebanon, wheat from chaff, privilege from his walking
like Hambone who's palsied, demented and living on the streets, used
to love somebody long gone.   *Hey, Hambone; Hey, Daddy*   she calls as

he passes, as she sits there sucking those tasty hard things
without a bone to pick with anyone: no   whalebone, ivory, no
Hambone in a hurry
to meet bones assembling in the valley for Jason and Ezekiel,
sowed teeth giving rise to armed skeletons   pushing up

like botanical freaks, beanstalks, the bones pulling themselves
together until a million march on the day of the dead wearing
turbans and hives, turbans and hives
to help him win back his sweetheart.   *Hey, Honey.*

She stirs a big old pot with a long bone
all indigo to the level of the dye, a liquid muscle
rushes madly in a circle, writing (with the superb ink
of her belief) that those who love bones prevail
after waiting for flesh, weaker by the hour, to give way

to Bones: simple rhythm instrument, two parts
held between the fingers of one hand and clacked together. She'd love
for him to play bones for her, just for her.   *Hambone, please
love the one you're with.   Don't end up*

6.
making castanets from a skull as did the Hatchet Man
who was later convicted, but somewhere out there

are castanets that aren't really castanets.

Somewhere out there also: catacombs, decay, decay, half-
lives, promises, a finger on a string to help a more perfect knot
come into being   on Wilma's wedding day, marriage to bone,
faithful, uncompromising truthful bone
                    —the mind cheats, soft
and dreaming, inventing words bone can't say, not even a simple
forensics-defying word: *race.*

Juniper Tree of Knowledge

A wife prayed for a baby as she peeled an apple
under a juniper tree and cut her finger, the sight of blood
confirming she was not pregnant.

But she was, as if the tree gave her a little something-something
for feeding its roots her blood (rewards are also meted out
by the alien plant in *Little Shop of Horrors).*

Perfection: A tree, an apple, a husband to tell of her desire
to procreate, her knowledge of her readiness. No surprises
until the sight of her baby is so magnificent it kills her.

She's buried, as she wanted, under the tree, where the oil
of the juniper preserves her body. Underground
she grows lovelier, her beauty becomes so strong it seems
destined to return although it doesn't; this loss is real.

There is not a widower in the woods for long. Rustling leaves make
him long for skirts rustling as they lift to permit consummation. He
marries a woman well-past first apples; she has a daughter to be sister
to her new step-son who has the qualities best

in a young woman who because of them can climb
from echelon to echelon (as wife): red as blood, white as snow.
He seems too perfect to have a father, certainly does not
need a mother. She calls the death of his mother *matricide.*

The boy is in her way, interferes with her transformation
of shrine to *her* home, *her* herbs altering the air, *her* curtains
filtering the light, *her* spinning wheel hypnotizing
the new family into forgetting the old. She must assert

her touches. But that is not enough. Somehow women will resort
to apples. This woman has a chest of them, result of days and days
of gathering until the smell of the stages of ripening and rot
overtakes the cottage. It makes the step-son forget

his step-mother's resentment and diurnal refusal to give him an apple
when he comes home from school. The apple trees are all
picked clean; he's at the mercy of her merciless stash. This day
he forgets that generosity from her is a warning; *of course*

you can have an apple; help yourself. Then the lid of the apple chest
decapitates him. For a moment the step-mother just looks
and admires the success of that old hunger: the power of *Winesap,*
Macintosh, Jonathan hers to pull down with a slot machine lever:
jackpot, jackpot, jackpot.
There's no bleeding (and that's just more luck).

This can be explained.
She positions the body at the table, applies a little mortar to the neck
and fixes the head upon it, ties a silk scarf around the neat scar
and waits for her daughter to come home and ask (hasn't yet missed a day)
to give her brother an apple; she loves him deeply
so does not question her mother's miraculous permission.
Thinking the apple will be a welcomed first gift

Marie is distressed that the dead boy refuses it; it's good enough; she's
good enough, and she follows her mother's advice to slap him
if he refuses again, to kingdom come. Obedience: his head
falls to the floor, and her guilt flies everywhere. She's killed her brother
and her father's delight, everything is promised to him
and she's no fit alternative although politeness falls from her tongue
as if nothing else is there; she never says but that she killed him

and how wrong she was even if his had been a tyrannical presence
—no other boy had no lust at all. As mothers must, this one helps
her daughter; no body, no murder; no murder, no punishment.

       They make soup

and serve the father heaping bowls of John. He slurps and tosses finger bones
and cuneiform bones of the foot under the table. Such tender meat. Not what the kings

and gods eat, but the kings and gods in the pot. In no time, tibia, femur, and plate cleaned
to make room for a wink at his new wife who has caught and skinned a bear. He'll boast
of that and all will be afraid to ever challenge either one of them; she caught a bear
and he caught her. John soup is the best soup he's ever had. She can cook too.

More, more
and soon his wife licks the spoon, her only and the last taste. He ate it all. Marie rocks
the bones under the table, kisses phalanges, and they do taste good, how can they taste good?
So much crying she seems to make more soup. *It is good enough to make you cry*
Father agrees. Finally: *Where's John?* Working, studying, visiting
his sick aunt, seeking his fortune, becoming a man—any one or all of these.

Marie wraps the bones in silk and drags them to the juniper tree, buries them one
by one, loves John more than ever, his bones dazzling in moonlight,
each one a wand. She writes his name in the air and it stays there, insects
holding it in place; she reads it in the clear ink of sudden rain inscribing her face,
and it's the message in the slime trail of snails—juniper branches
sign it, wind weeps it, feathers dry it and the bird begins the next day

singing about a step-mother who's wife and self-taught butcher, who's framing
her own daughter for the homicide, and feeding her own step-son to his father.
What a catchy song, no other bird has sung it; it speaks of indecency but with such
sweetness—impossible, but they hear it; all who hear it sing it too, finding they know it
by heart instantly; all its harassment, intolerableness, and beauty

that they follow to the cottage where the bird first acknowledges innocence
with a gold chain for the father and red shoes for Marie that teach her
how to dance again, then the step-mother, trying to run from the burning house
that is her own skin, is greeted with a millstone the bird drops, the sweetness aching
to break her neck, fracture her skull, and make her food

for the condors and vultures. Marie and Father watch them eat
(the miracle is not over), joined by John who's resurrected in time for supper
that Marie rushes to fix; she has no time for grief, and the vultures
have done such a good job anyway of making grief unnecessary.

Last Chance for the Tarzan Holler

1. The season that precedes Dali's *Autumn Cannibalism*

This day, like all days,
is a day of reckoning.

Gretel has felt electricity before
while rebaking walls and repairing
the licorice roof,   scraping mold

off the stale door
of the loaf in which she rooms
since inheriting the bread house

from the one who died there; her
assistance with the suicide assists
her cruelty.   Humperdinck's
Rubylips, witch, bitch ≈ Gretel, baker, widower-maker

G is the mature audience
for the scene of the crime
of comfort in this warm chair

warm as a living thing.
Ruby warming herself
in the stove.

The end.
Aw; tell me more, Mommie,
dearest Medea.

2. Unity, Inc.

This time perhaps the current will follow the blue path
        of veins in arms cuffed in leather. Loop-the-loop, the

Rotor, amusement park centrifugal thrill, Blue Streak, once
         a monster coaster. Wet and Wild's giant water slide, big
splash of grief into Dali's *Premonition of Civil War,*
         accurate although war can not be suave, gracious, or able
to partake of Susan Smith's southern hospitality. Civil(ity).

Anguish has no edge: entrails, body parts, Ruby's ashes,
bones that remain rounded for everlasting womanhood,
bombs for which bare-breasted women modeled; anguish
is a *soft construction with boiled beans,* soft as kindness, soft
boys: Michael and Alex, strapped in safety seats like the one
in my car, a Century 2000 on which is written:
for the safety and comfort of Ansted Moss.
Every morning he recites this scripture
as we drive past a transformer, farms, the Huron River.

One of Susan's soft-lipped boys plunged
at the age I was for my first baptism, naked
under the white robe and not aware
of how much of my wet self
the preacher's hand covered. He was holy
and I was becoming that way. Last chance
for the Tarzan holler. Those boys too

are believers. Everyone believes something.
Susan Smith will get better, believe it or not.
Premonition of amnesia. She's not alone,

practitioners of Munchausen's syndrome by proxy
feed off sympathy for the sometimes fatal, dreamed up
pathologies of their children; does turned vixen maintained
by salt licks through winter until it is the season to hunt
them down like dogs with dogs, like dogs eating dogs
until they're all gone in a premonition of peace; no
more best friends, nepotism, parricide.   She's

not alone. Accompanies those heading
for abortion clinics. These

madnesses, these choices, a little off
the top versus complete make-over, back
to the drawing board of unlimited ideas
where Medea, Gretel are born. It is that easy.
I see everyone at the market, everyone at
the clinic. And they see me. It is
that necessary. Breathe
a little easier for ten minutes

then the Mazda sinks.

—Cells, those drawings torn
out of animated existence are cels; how
I hate homonymity, as if I am singularly composed
of wicked artistry.

3.   Knock, knock.
         Who's there?
         Marrow.
         Whose marrow?

Zaynah is a girl whose match of bone marrow
may depend on boys dead in the water.

Her father loves her without this maudlin push
but after the press conference many others love her too,
including, he hopes, he pleads, the woman who adopted
Zaynah's first cousins when for their safety and comfort
they were removed from risk, maternal as that risk was;

they may be the bearers of the soft, fatty, vascular interior
of bones, collaborators in a life blood-postulated.

Gretel's wicked matriarchy.

>Knock, Knock.
>Come in, says the oven.
>But you don't even know who's there!
>Doesn't matter.
>Ah, a paragon of equal opportunity.

In that other house of bread where deacons serve it
all cut up, there is after the light one
a heavy supper of beans, squash, and pork chops.
The cooks sit hot in folding chairs by doors
and windows propped open with hymnals, and suck
a sweet intensity
from well-blackened bones of swine.

There is nothing between life and death, solid
and liquid forms of equivalent sacredness. Between
us, grudges.
>Just like *that!*
you're in John D. Long Lake
that does not know a day in which light
does not skim it like a wing,

especially on the October day that a car,
though a chariot is preferred, released two boys,
spirit willing, from their bodies so they could

sink into homecoming, alive
in comfortable seats
that can withstand collisions at 50 mph
if fastened properly—as they were. Susan's

marrow is eligible; Zaynah's life
could depend on the charity of the one
whose marrow is innocent, who did not put
her hands on her own marrow, did
not masturbate, was molested
although, knock, knock, these days
who wasn't?

Susan, I don't mean to be cruel
but as you know it is   inevitable. She

once took the boys on a picnic near water
cool and effervescing with motherhood
that blew bubbles that emerged
from Michael's right ear when she whispered
in his left, a rummage

of secret disappointments in school, so much
to remember, fix; life imprisoned in ego. Susan
likes Mr. Quixotic, *psst, pass it on—does not—does too*
and wants the time of day from shrugging shoulders,
silhouette

like iron monument in the park. They date
in her dreams and she's the Florence Nightingale
of Hadleyville and Roanoke that someone—Michael
(her son or the angel?)—said she couldn't be, kissing
away hurt until her lips rot

with duty and her ankles swell into cast iron casts,
weighing her down with identity—who did she marry?
Why isn't the love of her new life here under
bandages that she, the Arachne of Hadleyville and Roanoke,
wrapped into parcel, care package saved
for all the rainy days it takes to make a lake?

She kept her eyes on the loophole
in her wedding ring, so where's her Houdini?

Talcum and corn starch fill the air
as Gretel flails trying to escape a bathtub
turned to pudding, trying to escape

the revenge of marrow.

Ant Farm

One summer day
I took a kettle of steaming water and flooded an ant hill, watched as balled black bodies
floated down my brewed Nile and dried in the sand looking sugared, cinnamon-crusted.
I should have baked them into cookies and become famous for indecipherable
irresistible taste, a certain *je ne sais quoi.* Or thought to serve them poached. This
annihilation was not annihilation; the ants did not suffer and were turned into sugar beads
and their floating was serene.   I didn't know there'd be few

survivors; I expected in insects stamina a backbone obfuscates,
keeping vertebrates upright and vulnerable, subject to arrogance, breakage,
ravages, paralysis, the ideal immobility of food, facilitating admonishments to eat
until bones are picked clean, not only piranhas eating their instinct, but families
in public: Red Lobster, Bill Knapps, Kentucky Fried, countless rib joints, clean
as ivory; meals conclude with skeletons.   I admire teeth, the cutting

of the first one long before there can be any controlling of the bowels, a first pair
center front, vegetarian before that fulfillment; meat's indigestible until the fontanels
seal fate. Fetus eats as if entirely an embryonic flower, through root and stem called cord.
In the slits fanning around the navel like the possibility of petals
are dark slivers reminiscent of ants without their legs and my first boyfriend's
delight.   I killed them

although I had an ant farm sitting by my bed, such a narrow world it was, pressed between
sheets of Plexiglas no bigger than standard issue composition paper on which
I took notes on their progress that in my notebook never was, for I kept looking
at them from my perspective had I been as restricted; they could not open the world, reach
for stars though their tunnels longed to be telescopes.
Could not use a mirror's condolences to double their impression of space, so busy, busy,
carrying on their drudgery to distract them from escaping, even an ant queen
who could not fly away to mate with a marked man, but one day, her wings

were discarded, as they should be after the nuptials, at the opening to a tunnel, like a set
of tiny lips, white such as what, at the time, I thought happened, the bleaching, if arsenic
was kissed, but it happens too when there's too much confectioner's sugar
on what is consumed, and usually, when consumption takes place, there's too much
something, what, of course, varies so that sooner or later, everything has a turn being vice.

Outside, trophallaxis keeps ants going, reciprocal feeding, exchange of chemical
stimulation, workers (wingless, infertile females denied or uninterested in sex) tend
the young, feeding them honeydew from raids on aphids and giving other luscious stuff
of their own feeding to larvae whose surfaces secrete a substance more luscious that
these females crave, and thus, work even harder for the high, the all-consuming high,
the paradisiacal reward although these busy ants are neither saved nor unsaved nor
concerned.   A group of lactating women assemble in a suburban park, get high together as
their babies nurse. Feelings some of them

don't get from spousal intimacy. Some fancy ants are living honey pots, workers,
through whatever awareness is possible in formic nervous systems, who know themselves
sublime as they are fed unbearable quantities of honeydew, and they must wonder whether
or not they are deserving of overwhelming pleasure though none complain, accepting a
blessed fate that nevertheless restricts their options. Then these females, rather ideally
nunnish, gorged to a real inedia, lose their ant form, becoming butterballs round as the
cosmos and becoming the cherubic sustainers of the colony, releasing sweet drops as
needed yet remaining full, complete. Diva ants.

The boyfriend who lived near water let ants crawl along his arms, then he would flick them
off, quickly kicking his leg, trying to catch them in his pants cuff. He became good
at this. Too good to forget.

There are close to five thousand species of ants, among them the Cameroonian
stink ant capable of producing a sound audible to humans, especially to women
full of milk who are so sensitive to crying, a frail decibel makes milk flow just as our
desperation is supposed to touch God to the point that he can't help but dispense remedies,
sometimes in code, to what has become his own misery. The stink ant feeds from the rain
forest floor and in just trying to survive, which is when everything happens, during
attempts at survival, sometimes inhales a fungal spore that survives in the ant's brain,
reproducing and controlling, using the ant as its slave wagon for transport to prominence
at the top of a fern, a pinnacle like a spear and the ant that knows of its disgrace,
despite the take-over of its brain, clamps its mandibles to the spear so that it seems
impaled, sort of an act of hara-kiri, and dies as the spore now flourishes, consuming
the totality of the dead meat; death graciously allows for less grievous consumption, more
open relish, and in two weeks, the time it takes for a woman to miss a period after
fertilization, a spike with a tip orange as sunset begins to emanate

from the former head of the ant, and upon reaching an inch and a half of success, triggers fireworks, an explosion of spores descending from the heights and looking for a sponsor.   There's an ant like this in Florida where you could be in love, foolish, getting pregnant in grass on which some of these dead ants are fastened by their jaws. I was told not to eat watermelon seeds, that vines and snakes would grow within me, so after eating them, I took Castoria, the whole bottle of that gentle laxative for children, although I knew, for the color betrayed it, that Castoria was made by liquefying ants, that ants were farmed just to purge.

Ear

It is called the incomplete human flower, I know because I have called it that,
usually right before sex, when everything looks good. *You keep bringing me flowers,*
my tongue says sliding into the fossae of his right ear's helix and anti-helix
shown at left without my tongue.

Lacking one of those pretty and slim proboscides of certain avuncular bugs
(you know, the men keeping company with never-married mamas, too familiar
not to have a family title but most definitely not anybody's fathers) cruising
the flower beds needing a dose of hepatica or burst of the stench of rotting fish
and burnt sugar that the eight-feet tall lily *Amorphophallus titanum* of the Sumatran
jungle emits in a strength to knock a man flat out and take from carrion beetles
that last drop of resistance that was their whole blood, I can't get in

the internal ear's labyrinth, neither the osseous nor the membranous labyrinth
within the other, yet here is where sound happens, where that which means
to be heard must travel vestibule, canals, and cochlea to the mecca
of the auditory nerve. The body is nothing but tunnels, made for excavation, covert opera-
tions, ergo my tongue, this ear I want to pluck and pin to my lapel, wear it
as well as he does; no, better and both of them, one to wear above, beside, on

each breast, and he could speak right in them somehow speaking to all of me
of Calvoli Island where gulls, of the western point, kitsch their nests with:
bones, feces, regurgitated seafood, dead chicks and addled eggs and the gratitude
of blowflies accepting such lavish invitation to flourish, prosper.
Pampered they are indeed (as is this ear), and giddy, as gull excrement and stink
compete with putrescence of a flower, *Helicodiceros muscivorus,* an arum lily
presenting, for the blowflies' pleasure, a spathe color of decomposing meat and just
as fetid as *a well-matured sheep-sized corpse*   so that

it's no contest; arum and blowflies have the orgy, flies pursuing *a dark, damp*
and particularly fetid aperture with which to mate, and that exists within the lily's
dark chamber past the neck and spadix, a space from which the flies do not escape,
the presence ilking up with humidity, rot-based arousal such as never known,
causing eggs to erupt from those places lust-distended on the insects, ova offered
for these services instead of cash, piling up as if a stripper has been fully plastered
with green. Naturally, maggots hatch, such is the intensity and odor, but perish without

real meat, real decomposition although for the parents, there is nectar of the flower
besides nectar of their erotic throes, and they are helpless to it, suck it up without
the howling my man likes to hear from me as a continuously updated status report
on his work. The morning after or morning after that, male flowers
give the pollen bath that releases those flies that have not suffocated
to *Sardinian sunlight* bright as approval so into the next lily inflorescence they rush
before this palace is shut down by an agricultural vice squad

just as sometimes he is deaf to all but Dow Jones, NASDAQ,
the numbers getting in deep, but I can add, multiply, divide and divide endlessly;
I can fuck with the numbers.

Crystals

In 1845 Dr. James Marion Sims had seen it many times,
vesico-vaginal fistula, abnormal passageway
between bladder and vagina through which urine leaks
almost constantly if the fistula is large

as it tends to become after those pregnancies
not quite a year apart in Anarcha and her slave
friends Lucy, Betsey. *If you can just fix this*
the girl said, probably pregnant again, her vulva inflamed,
her thighs caked with urinary salts; from the beginning
he saw his future in those crystals.

Society women sometimes had this too, a remaking of the vulva,
more color, pustules like decorations of which women
were already fond: beads, cultured pearls of pus, status.
Perhaps the design improves in its greater challenge to love
and fondle even in the dark except that there is pain,
inability to hold water.

He tried to help Anarcha first, drawing on what
he was inventing: frontier ingenuity and gynecology,
and operated thirty times, using a pewter teaspoon
that he reshaped, bent and hammered for each surgery,
no sterilant but spit, while she watched; it became
his famous duck-bill speculum too large and sharp
to be respectful, yet it let him look.

Such excoriation, such stretching of the vaginal walls, tunnel
into room; such remembrance of Jericho, prophecy of Berlin
when his mind was to have been on her comfort and healing.

Through the vulva was the way most tried to access her
yet they did not come close.   Using

a half-dollar he formed the wire suture that closed
Anarcha's fistula on the thirtieth, it bears repeating, thirtieth
attempt.

For the rest of her life she slept in the Sims position:
on her left side, right knee brought to her chest; she so long,
four years, on his table came to find it comfortable, came to find
no other way to lose herself, relieve her mind,
ignore Sims' rising glory, his bragging in the journals
that he had seen the fistula *as no man had ever seen it before.*
Now they all can.

Anarcha who still does not know anesthesia except
for her willed loss of awareness went on peeing as she'd
always done, just not so frequently and in reduced
volume, hardly enough for a tea cup, but whenever
necessary, the doctor poked, prodded, practiced

then, successful, went gloved and shaven to help ladies
on whom white cloths were draped; divinity
on the table to indulge his tastefulness.

It should be noted
that Anarcha's fistula closed well,
sealed in infection, scarred
thickly

as if his hand remained.

A Hot Time in a Small Town

In this restaurant a plate of bluefish pâté
and matzos begin memorable meals.

The cracker is ridged, seems planked, an old wall
streaked sepia, very nearly black
in Tigrett, Tennessee

where it burned

into a matzo's twin. While waiting
for a Martha's Vineyard salad, I rebuild the church
with crackers, pâté as paste

as a flaming dessert arrives at another table where diners
are ready for a second magnum of champagne; every day
is an anniversary; every minute, a commemoration
so there is no reason to ever be sober

to excuse incendiaries who gave up the bottle,
threw alcohol at the church, spectacular reform

in flames themselves ordinary—there'd been fire in that church
many times, every Sunday and even at the Thursday
choir rehearsals. For years there'd been a fired-up congregation

so seething, neighborhoods they marched through ignited
no matter their intention; just as natural as summer.
There were hot links as active as telephone lines
whose poles mark the countryside as if the nation is helpless
without a crucifix every few yards; pity they are combustible

and that fire itself is holy, that its smoke merges with atmosphere,
that we breathe its residue, that when it is thick and black enough
to believe in, it betrays and chokes us; pity
that it is the vehicle that proves the coming of the Lord,
the establishment of his kingdom, his superiority because

fire that maintains him disfigures us; when we try to embrace
him; we find ourselves out on a limb   burning. The meal

tastes divine, simply divine
and I eat it in the presence of a companion dark as scab,
as if skin burned off was replaced as he healed
with this total-body scab

under which he is pink as a pig, unclean at least
through Malachi.

In my left hand,   a dash of Lot's wife; in my right, a mill
to freshly grind the devil; since fire is power
both the supreme good and supreme evil are entitled
to it; most of the time, what did it matter
who was in charge of Job?   Both burnt him.

Glory

The sun does not really rise; the earth turns and leans
into that perception as it circles a sun busy burning
for the sake of light.

That's what I'd like God to do, burn himself again
for the sake of light. Commit to the bush instead of vacating
when it got too hot, berries burning the hands picking them,
picking Him, Moses suffering heat as they suffer in a Chicago August,
five hundred dropping, no rapture to sustain them, members
of Star of Hope.   There should be more hot etching of stone,
more coal-dark hair burning to gray ash for descent
from Sinai and ego, more wheels to take us for a hot time
in Ezekiel's town of exile along the river Chebar.

There's nothing   like burning, the changes it induces,
transformations that are not subtle,   gross advantages
the least of which is light.   The body, always a problem, remade.
This form is ideal for this life and no other.

Fire has taken many   before their sacrifice
was understood; most days no one wakes smeared
with ashes of Saint Joan.   And most only dream, a vaporous
smoky act, of walking the coals in Suva, neem leaves
on their heads, thoughts cooking, passion igniting.

We know what they were, many of them, not necessarily
their names, but they didn't burn because of name alone that is weaker
than identity, even when name   claims it.   Instead
a holy hotness was subverted, furnaces raged
with contention and contagion; putrid ideology reached
a boiling point and sizzled so that it seemed relieving to burn
them all, take their teeth, hair and money, but even burned
they stayed chosen   by faith in something glorious that smoke
became a witness to, lusty and strong;   testimony is fire.   Fire
is alive; needs air, feeds, grows.

Occupied houses sometimes go up in flames; yes, the body is such
a structure.   Sati is such a ritual for widows.   Charring of skin
is not meant to thrill or it would not repulse so many.   But some marvel
at anything bright so intensely do they crave the luminous.

On the whole we are marvelous beings
the way we can adapt and accept such awfulness
as there is everywhere, mixed in, of course,
with what we really want to see: jugglers and safe crossings
on the high wire as narrow as most hope is.

Combustion likewise is marvelous, when the blaze
is spirit ever expanding, enacting   some incredible reaching
before firefighters arrive to condemn something
it is a pity to destroy.   There is disappointment
in water mastering glory thought too mighty to be extinguished
but this is not a defect in glory; it is a defect in water.

Now is the ascent of smoke, dark formlessness
suggesting the totality of wretchedness on the horizon
as it spreads and simulates incredibly localized nighttime
focused as are lasers and guilt.

Elijah rode a column of smoke to paradise, and to Oz,
a girl rode one that turned; what was it burned
to make those vehicles?
Women burned for witchcraft, the treason red hot
and only smoke when it was over, wisps, fine and thin
as silk's ambition. Burned for what was probably only
pre-menstrual syndrome or the effects of eating ergot-contaminated
rye bread.   Shadrach, Meshach, and Abednego would
not burn; nor St. Agnes, for whom the fire parted; *whatever water
can do, I can do better,* fire said, content to tickle them.
They missed a chance to be fireworked.

Give yourself to the glory raging
if the moment comes in your lifetime.
Give yourself to the astronomical temperature   where there's
instant outburst into flame, the warmest, the ultimate hospitality.
I don't mean to say embrace it, but if it looks when it detonates
like glory, then take no chances, fellowship

with what little colored boys know
lashed and gasolined on the branches, imperfect crosses
with all the limbs intact, the wood undisciplined, the boys
a wild offering and given to God who could use them
since he's not the God he was in the past when he rejected certain
burnt offerings, clad his favorites in asbestos, outfitted the others
in salt; now he takes whatever he's given, revision into neuter
in the Oxford *inclusive language* new testament
without old biases, without tradition, and without passion.

This much is unchanged: smoke seeks
upward motion and the moment it starts to rise
it's redeemed into atmosphere.   I know
that people are combustible, property of glory.
I tell you there's hope for us
and it's all in our ability to burn.

Second Grade Art: The Stunning Chances

It could be those terrors more apparent at seven
than at any other time, shadow of needle-nose pliers
meant only to install stereo system, speaker wires
that carry Bach and sweetness
to ears that model one of the shapes of torment
                              but all the forms of grace;   instead

she dares sky and struggle to cross the lines drawn between them. As yet
no blue seeps into the manila void known as demarcation
that refutes the world shifting in her kaleidoscope, lovely but unstable, con-
vulsive, sway and give even in buildings tall as stacked trees, their concrete
roots mingling with bedrock as if they're fundamental

and not monstrosity. The persistence of her brushes scraping nearly
depleted shallow beds of her watercolors gives her the chance to stroke
the canvas of a detached ear that stroking reveals
is a misshapen swan's neck or a whole cygnet contorted for the egg
the way she and everything else are contorted for the world. The chance

to care for the shunned and isolated part as one day she might care for
a breast removed so that it can't kill although there's no longer that hope
of milk, that form of Bach, terror and sweetness as the liquid locates
all the bumpy possibilities of the tongue. She has already

cared for each feather found, some black and successful
from calamus almost all the way to completion, white only at the tip
unlike her father's worried hair. With them, she's made a bird
whose flight she improvises, beginning to understand what

should not be understood—feathers attached to a cast of an ear
whose severance rejects the Bach rising like steam from dew
evaporating into misery when solace again each day becomes vagrant

—only hobos almost kept up with it, and she hardly sees them anymore
or their trains that rust now in their dead stops; she was child in a time that's
now too old to have children, a time whose mechanical fascinations

have had to accept that their turn is over although it seems
there wasn't a chance to play because there wasn't;   instead

there are trips to see the fat world Baby Flo makes, the girl assumes,
by eating, an insatiable hunger to possess sanity, sweetness, solace by eating
up the plagues, tormenting decadence of what tastes so good, it is craved
beyond addiction—her savior after eating all sinful deliciousness
in one awful gulp is too skinny to believe.   Daddy rushes her by church

to five hundred warm pounds of woman whose scent is so delicate
it disappears after first notice leaving the girl skeptical for a minute
—which seems to be but probably isn't for the best.   Baby Flo's ears
are small as if Baby Flo selects what gets in, only Bach

and occasionally a lesser compliment such as this girl's
nearly believable comment about the brown necklaces
Baby Flo's folds of skin make, the bottom one a brown collar
as proper as Miss Dove's. *Good morning, Miss Baby Flo,*
the girl says, candy lipstick in her hand, dimes in her loafers,
a little tissue in her Lovable trainer

because doubt has managed to prevail

(despite the presence of a woman who really is as big as a temple
the girl has been trying to draw without pen and ink asking questions

that prohibit the seizing of this stunning chance of being lost
not only in Baby Flo's unprecedented opportunity for a heyday of disease
considering the magnitude of the province, but, more importantly, also

in this stunning chance of eternity surrendering
to Baby Flo's undeniable wisdom of flesh)

Overseeing the Cherry

I love them too and was one
of the little girls on swings, ice skates, dresses opening
to display Fruit of the Loom overseeing the cherry, for just a second, the brevity
that proves the truth of the moment and the accident of truth.
It is said
that in a man that is maternal too much has gone awry
to rehabilitate him. That Peter Pan still plays doctor.
That he may be neat, pubic hair combed, tied with a bow.
He may be almost anyone. The accusation will stick anywhere.

Blessed are the pure in heart, the low in spirit
and subjects of the rumors, the co-owners
of the history of deviancy.

It is a form of love, in the same category as what
even popes accept though decline to practice. It happened
in moonlight so kisses were appropriate, good night and good night
again   as he tucked youngsters into himself, romantic it seemed
to those spying from afar, aboard spaceships and fantasies.

There is a three-year-old sleeping whose breath floats
in jasmine to my room and leads me to his bedside
where my breath is unrestrained and eager to swallow him
though it is quickly dominated by his nostrils and he is Cupid
in bed and there is no choice except to let him cook my breath
to the consistency of wax even when it falls on him and burns
the easy rest, his arm shadowed on the sheets like a wing until
he moves it waking from dream he does not articulate but that surely
was more wonderful   given the loveliness of his head
than this presence dark and insomniac in the room.

Whatever I am, even the one
who scarcely mothered Jesus, kneeling before him
as shepherdess buying the right for lamb to represent him
and chew the circumcised foreskin,   it is no monster

I've brought into the world, but something beyond my genes and proteins,
for they are just alibi; yet if through my tight space, then
humble he is, if not human.
For the pedophile, one kiss
and the gardens and palaces of delight vanish
giving rise to the monster
and others also moon-begotten: werewolf
and vampire heeding the white oracle all night long;
deeply pious and men   underneath their devotion.

After Reading *Beloved*

It's just a question of   when,
right after unprotected sex with: strangers,
the boy who loves eternally instantly, a husband,
a husband's friends

or as soon as the first blood appears
on the cotton crotch of the Pam undies
knowing how three drops led to the thought
that led to the birth of Snow White and
the devastation of all her caretakers

or can any time become the right time to control
or revoke a birth as on that episode of *M.A.S.H.*
where the Korean woman swallowed all instinct
to save those on a bus from soldiers trained, like
our soldiers, to overcome reverence?

Need ruined everything; the child screamed
for itself, for its mother, and as soon as it affirmed
its life, the mother's hand clamped tightly against lips
and nose small as a bud.
                              We know what the atom can do;
Eve pulled down that first red one, split it with her teeth
and survived. We still survive termination, not all of us
but enough to ruin eugenics, politics, sport, and convenience.

Some termination may be necessary to prove this:
The mother on the bus suffocated her baby, refusing
the gas that suspended the consciousness of chickens
because she thought her breast could do it better.
Sometimes it can until well after weaning, and by then,
someone else did it for salvation; Mary did not have to wield
the hammers forcing in nails slightly rounded like her nipples.

A Man

How handsome he was, that man who did not court
the girls fawning all over him as if he'd already saved them,
it's my leg, one said, raising her hem as she'd raised it in dreams
he knew of, for everything reached him as prayer, *my leg, Sir,*
is not perfect although as he looked, it glistened and the blood
became more productive. He did not date, nor rendezvous in tunnels and tents,
did not kiss except to heal, did not harass, malign nor mutilate;
threw no stones

        and he was a man; never forget that he was a man,

that being a man improved him. Before the mothering, He was a solo act
ramming omnipotence down the throats of Ramses, Job, all the sinning nobodies
of Sodom. He was feared before he was born a triplet of flesh completing
the one vaporous, the other heavy and strict; now he's desirable, vulnerable;
in the mother he visited stages of: fig, fish, pig, chicken, chimp   before settling irrevocably
on a form more able to strive. This was a more significant time in darkness,
gestation of forty weeks, than three days in a hillside morgue; he learned maternal heartbeat
and circulation of her blood so well they became dependency,
and so he learned that some radiance is not his, hers

came in large part just from being Mary—how content she was even before pregnancy,
betrothed, blushing to ripen the fields; content even before she knew of angels,
and now, with this mound of baby, she was parent of a world whose prospering
she encouraged, activity of fish, magma, sulfur, the earth striving
        just as she did.

He was a man
          yet the usher of miracles, preaching on a mountain
where reverberation gave him the power of five thousand tongues, yet not
a big man, not athletic, ordinary looking except for that glow and doves circling
him in the desert, doves that had been vultures earning their transfiguration
by consuming decaying meat just as he ate all the sin; for that flattery, he bid them dip
their feathers in his eye, drawing into them that sweet milk around the iris.

He was a man

when he began to understand love, erasing the lines between
Gentile, Jew, and invited any who wanted to come to his father's house for bottomless milk,
honey, ripe fruit, baskets of warm bread and eggs, wine, live angels singing. Weary revelers
could lay their heads on his breast, he said, needing intimacy; he thinks
as a man, therefore

                                    he is a man
and good times, memories can be
adequate heaven. He knows the distance a man
is from his father, how likely it increases till the deathbed; he knows

what a man knows

the now and here, and can be called by name,
and can be wounded, and must struggle, and must be proud
every now and then or could not continue, must be worth something,
must be precious to himself and preferably to at least one other, must be,
in these thousands of post-Neandertal years, improving, must have
more potential, becoming not only more like God, but more like
what God needs to become, so moves also,
so God moves also

        because a man moves.

Cheating

The cheating belongs to a season that can not be resurrected.
And each spring has memory so is not original.   I know only
of how it was for Lazarus and that account from a man
who had no real cheating to explain.   Cheating death
is honorable.

When Lazarus left his tomb the way I left the house that day,
entirely too casual for what was happening, he did not bring with him
a trail of bees and flowers to show the depth of summer; he did not
shiver the chill of transition, rays of light crinkling
behind him to suggest the imminence of snow somewhere
in the world. The season of Lazarus
is unknown and gone.
                              He was called, but was not called again;
he died at least twice and knew injustice, believed the first—and last
it turned out—calling was a promise; in faith, he was willing
to die endlessly, to enter into contract and die just so the caller
could call and become known for calling, but the dependency
was not balanced; Lazarus did all the needing, the caller, all
the cheating, unless, of course, the caller be called God; that
name-calling changes the picture; lucky Lazarus, alive
to fear God again.

But that is too big to really matter; most of living is
small and unimportant, uninspiring. In this case, for instance,
it was a musician's way of asserting that I was the only woman
in the world though we sat in a cafeteria, the deep fat smelling tooled
and seductive, pointing to seams in the cow girled server's hose
as platters came close to our noses.   Then
he brushed strands of hair away from my eyes
as if brushing away bits of eraser
after making the picture of me perfect.

This isn't the time to wonder just what it was
I did for him in 1975, a season gone and increasingly
insignificant; we came together as any strangers can.

What allows some strangers to go past strangeness, exchanging
what is called depth although no depth of human understanding
or intelligence has been indisputably proven? Mostly it is as if
I don't care about the world, for most of its population
consists of strangers; it is as if I welcome their losses for fulfilling
the day's quota of loss so that my day may be sweet and frivolous,
but the musician and I did more; we allowed vulnerable connections,
spoke of dreams about to evaporate unless we breathed life
on them for each other, as if spousal breath would be inadequate
in its familiarity, as if I knew a husband could no longer console who had
once cheated on me because he didn't really know me or himself or
the limitations of living, the truth of human inadequacy

that we accept the way finally we accept our age, and understand that coupling
is entirely choice, not mandate; that in chemistry, any atoms of hydrogen
and oxygen will partner into water, that widows survive and still
have moments of happiness; reproduction isn't even necessary, the world
is not only for our species or necessarily for any species at all, the dead Jupiter
and Neptune go on rotating and revolving without audience or chronicler; Earth
can survive without us; our purpose is not maintenance of the world
but of ourselves.   Any two

can wed or cohabit; we choose to be faithful, to cut ourselves off
from all other sources of pleasure and fulfillment, for life in its variety and profusion
assures that multiple compatibility is possible; we choose not to look for
the other perfect matches, the one in each million; we choose. My husband

is my Lazarus; I call him from the tomb where misery is everything.
It is all about suffering; that is what people do, suffer the trivialities
we have called important because they are ours and are all that we have,
among them our movies and investments, as if value is something other
than our own delusion; we are not

what has become of the pioneers and dreamers; they are dead and they
had no knowledge that could predict the likes of the world now; it
is a place they would not recognize, perhaps would not be able to cherish

although as its antecedents, they might try to claim credit, might want to believe
that they are somehow responsible for our progress, such as it is. These

lies do not cheat the truth; the truth is ever present and known,
but it is truth and therefore is undesirable in its immutability.
The truth is finished; it is not lovely architecture and is self-made
and is also the only originality, not expandable nor reducible
and really doesn't affect our lives, existing independently
and somewhere else, not in the board, court or class rooms, but nearby
and untouchable; our cheating does not disrupt it. Truth

actually has very little to do with life since it seems
to be the point of the grave, but if that is all that truth is, it is not
particularly useful; it is then too accessible to be useful.

from

SLAVE MOTH

(2004)

The Tennessee Prophet Beehive Project

Irene Perry, Peter Perry's grandmother, died yesterday,
sleeping on her grandson's porch, her mouth wide open
and so sweet of Tennessee whiskey
that it was full of bees when they found her.

Her tongue was so stung, so swollen
that Sully couldn't close her mouth. Bees
went in and out of her like crazy needles dancing
instead of stitching that mouth shut.
It was allowed for Sully to touch her dead, his
job, since he was a dwarf involved with all the dead,
mostly slave dead here and at the Staleys, the Cheston
and the Kelster farms, and animal dead not fit
for eating.

Doc Wallace Lonton said that
Irene must have been inviting the bees in for hours
because they had had time to set up a hive
in her throat
and turn some of her spit to honey
and tuck a queen in under Irene Perry's
thick quilt of a tongue.

She would have been left that way, the survivors
thinking on a miracle
except for the problem of a miracle
being served up by bees, and the problem of stingers
not being the acknowledged property of heaven
for being so much like the two points of the devil's
divided tongue,
but rot didn't stand for that anyway
and eventually got even more involved with the corpse
than the bees.
Rot didn't get there right away though;
Peter Perry's idea was faster. Beat grief, too.
He loved the hive Irene had become,

and the added spectacle
of a dwarf pursuing that mouth honey.
Albino Pearl filling the jugs.
Master Peter wrote up several signs
and invited people as far as Gallatin, Knoxville,
and Nashville, even got word to Roanoke,
to come see the miracle, come see the source
of his graces: a grandmother
who had become a fountain of honey.

The amazing, mystifying, miraculous honeyfying body
of Irene. The gold mine in every one of his pockets.

Too perfect to keep.

Come early
and see rivers of honey pour from her ears,

come fill
a jug with Perry Paradise Honey for a dollar.

He almost lost himself and nearly kissed me
he was so happy.

He forgot all about having to have a funeral.
Unless that's what all this spectacle was
(death of the last of the meaning of his marriage, too),
so many fine coins in Peter Perry's pockets.
Forgot to notify Aunt Baly-Belinda,
his grandmother's daughter-in-law.

Doc Wallace Lonton certified the death
and Rev. Lucious Adler (of the aristocratic Adlers
who made a fortune in whiskey, a family
into which Peter Perry's Aunt Baly-Belinda married,
wealth that therefore didn't touch Peter Perry directly

though he wanted it to, and tried to divert it
to himself just as he diverted that creek,
by being as sweet to Baly-Belinda as honey
and a son to her, called her *Aunt Mama* and everything);
Rev. Lucious Adler certified the miracle.

The certifier could tell that Irene's mouth
was open to praise and bless when the bees came in
like little angels in their best yellow-striped Sunday suits
and made the honey of heaven
that they were painting her soul with
and turning on the light of her soul with.
Rev. Adler called it the *Honeyfication of Irene*.

And that soon became the title of his most requested sermon.
(Peter Perry felt he was entitled to a percentage
of the collection on those Sundays, seeing as his own
Irene made possible Rev. Adler's fame.)

Some of the honey sticking to the little angel bee legs
rubbed off on Irene's tobacco-brown teeth
as the angel bees flew in and out
of Irene's transfigurating honeyfying body
and gave her teeth the appearance of each one of them
being a gold-rimmed, pearly, tobacco gate.

Angels touched you without being seen,
luna moths flew into the cabin, my dream of freedom
acting as a flame. I could feel the tails of luna hind wings
tickling my eyelids, but by the time I opened my eyes
they were gone.

They woke you up before the day got up
so you could splash cold spring water on your face
like you were being saved every morning

like you were waking up to a new world
and the only sound was a bird's sound,
only hammer was a woodpecker's
and that was all the time you got to be a person
because in a minute came the rest of it.

Varl, you heard *Varl,* and it was the magic word
that turned you back to slave.

Perry angels were bees. Varl angels
were luna moths. Desperation was both of ours.

Heaven in hives; heaven in cocoons.

More of it in the gold mines in his pockets.
Also his golden curiosity helping him see gold in me.

Peter Thomas Perry married Ralls Janet
when I was about five years old
(I don't remember much about the wedding
and now I'm about the age she was
when she married him) just for a dowry
which was mostly the prestige of marrying a Heffring
(she the prestige of getting closer to Adler money)
but since the wedding, the Heffrings have lost
almost everything but their color—and Ralls Janet lost
more of her flimsy hold on her husband—crop
and livestock sickness cleaned up their big farm pastures
and orchards to just sunlit, moonlit glow,
deformed all their plans; Ralls Janet
had once been a Heffring queen, had ruled; everything
gone except some faith, I suppose, which was mighty
difficult to put in a bank and was a paltry inheritance, too,

considering, for instance, that Jessper had more faith

(things would change, slavery might end in her lifetime)
than Peter Perry and Ralls Janet combined,
yet Jessper wouldn't ever take that enormous faith
and run with it to a place where faith and freedom
meant the same real thing
instead of dependency on miracles.

Rev. Adler was involved with whiskey, too,
but his involvement could be brought on entirely
by birthright and not sin
since he was born into the Adlers,
cousin to the founders of the Adler Distillery
and owners of the distillery's fortune that built
his magnificent church

where Dwarf Sully was two nights ago fixing the roof
that was damaged by gusts of wind that seemed
to take freedom more seriously than most of us.

Peter Perry's Aunt Baly-Belinda knew something
about freedom, too, about independence
and when she married into the Adlers, she set up
her nephew Peter as a supplier of some of
the distillery's grain, lifting Peter's spirit
(and his purse close to as much as he wanted
but he can't give up cotton, can't give up slaves, none
of his pleasure, can't give up a connection to Mamalee
as her master, only as her master, and through her,
reach me. He was a man of conviction but not of courage.
I saw him trying not to love Mamalee, see him now try harder
not to love me; I'm aware of how he tries, a middling effort,
not to prefer me in Ralls Janet's presence
over his wife with sunset-colored eyes,
the green obliterated. Sinking sun eyes).

All Adlers did some kind of spirit work, Sully said

but there were many kinds of spirits, and Mamalee
chided him for trying to link Rev. Adler to evil ones
for no reason other than the reverend's knowing Peter Perry
who was not actually any relation to the reverend;
for no reason than his not condemning slavery
from his pulpit

where he practiced the usual sermon while
Sully pounded usefulness and protection back
into the roof. "What does it matter, Sully?"
Mamalee asked the little man who loved her
but not secretly, but without guilt and shame,
who sometimes took her in his deformed arms;
"What does it matter?"
she repeated, "Rev. Adler doesn't keep any slaves.
He's nobody's master, not even his own. Ask him

and he'll tell you that *he* has a master, that *he*
is the Lord's slave. He's not important, Sully.
He's too weak to help. Only a weak man
has to hide behind the Lord so completely.
He says that slavery will end only when it's
the Lord's will. He never thinks

on how the Lord's will could be for somebody
to take action. Ask him how does he figure out
what is the Lord's will and what isn't. Ask him

and all he'll do is tell you that it's not the Lord's will
for him to know what is the Lord's will and what isn't
or he would know."

———

Reverend Moses Dunn out of Nashville
who came here for revival wouldn't have it.

Wouldn't be impressed with the angel bees.
He'd been stung, too,

and even though the stinging got him into preaching
he didn't praise or recommend it.

He called Irene Perry's bee hived mouth
the most ridiculous church he'd ever seen,
worse than in the uncivilized territories to the west
when he'd been, finding it too much trouble
to keep dust out of his Bible, so he was back for good,
on a narrower circuit.
Especially preaching in the mountains
with the echoes agreeing with and emphasizing every word.

He said you might as well call it miracle
when flies circle over carcasses
because in keeping to circles
the flies were acting out halos.
And the stink was just to make the miracle
conspicuous; if you had a nose you couldn't miss
such distinguished stinking.

And that meant any skunk was a prophet
of the church of the beehived mouth.

He was a preacher with as much a feel for life
as for heaven, and wouldn't stand for nonsense
in either one. Realistic, he was. Practical.
Not at all what Peter Perry usually liked.

Sully used to belong to Reverend Dunn
(who never married), cleaning up behind the horses
that Reverend Dunn brought right into the churches,
especially (of course) outdoor services

so that they would hear the preaching and be changed
into a Pegasus breed

even though there was never any sign of the change,
no transfigurating in the barn with bees making honey
in a horse neck or painting honey on horse teeth,
no reviving the dead with horse breath.

Traveling with Reverend Dunn
was how Sully had his legendary hundred children,
probably no more than six or seven, if that,
but he believed otherwise. So did Peter Perry,
the widened permissiveness of deformity.
I'd never seen any of them (as far as I knew)
but out of respect for Sully, I asked everyone
I met if they were a child of Sully.

Every time somebody told the story of Sully
especially when Sully told it himself
another child or two
was added on. It was as if Dwarf Sully was another Noah,
building something that would survive
the coming destruction
for which he was preparing
and getting a head start on replenishing the earth
with his own.

There were supposed to be a few little Dunns
across Kentucky, too. There'd be more than a few
if that story were told as much; it wasn't
Sully's favorite.

Sully had a master before Reverend Dunn,
up until Sully when he was just a child
grabbed hold of that master's gun
and twisted it around that master's neck

just as if gunmetal wasn't anything but a piece of rope

—believe if you want to, with Master Peter,
that Dwarf Sully charmed the gun, but even if you don't,
it was still built on the distorted truth of Sully catching
a whip in his teeth, and with his teeth, cracking the whip
and sending that master to the ground. Couldn't beat Sully.
The power, Peter Perry believed, of dwarfism.
The beating meant for Sully ended up
on whomever was trying to beat him.
He was protected by powers
no master could subdue

so that master, who was giving up his stony acres
and heading west where gold did the work of the sun,
sold Sully to Reverend Dunn for the price
of seeing the fear of God put in him,
though I don't believe that master has been paid yet.

Sully and Reverend Dunn were kind of friends
without trust; they liked each other fine enough
but shared no trust. Reverend Dunn preaching through
the country with a wise dwarf of Egypt on a horse
at his side. They had a near about perfect understanding
that was betrayed when Reverend Dunn
got to be good friends with Peter Perry
who took communion in the fields
and then Mamalee took it, too.
One bottle. One glass.

When Peter Perry's friendship with Reverend Dunn
was secure, the reverend traded his friend Sully
for a share of the corn crop after it became whiskey
and more communion. Peter Perry had to have
the dwarf. Would have sold his soul. The wagon loaded

up with bottles, Reverend Dunn drove down the roads
with the bottles making music banging into each other,
the joyful noise, Reverend Dunn said, of secular salvation.
He said that folk everywhere he went needed medicine.

Upon occasion, the bottles banged songs of escape
next to slave arms, legs, chests, necks also in the wagon.

Reverend was the man's name,
not his title. Folk assumed that since he was *Reverend*
that he was a real preacher, but Sully let on as to how
he never was. *Reverend* wasn't the name of his heart.
He was no closer to the Lord than anybody else was. If
he was a real preacher, he'd have to be Rev. Reverend Dunn,
just as Captain would have to be Cap. Captain

to take on title (but *name* is more than title
so isn't necessary for the man who is in command of his life
or for the man who saves himself already).

He insisted that Master Peter bury the beehive prophet.

And left right after explaining to Master Peter
why slaves endure "the splendid suffering
that the artifice of slavery is for. Heaven will regale
the triumph of their pain and will remove fully the scabs
they have worn over the entirety of their wounded skin.
Even you would agree, Brother Peter, that it will be a glorious sight
when the last scab is removed from the last Negro
who joins the rest of the healed in a stupefying marvel
that during all that time slaving,
his white skin was busy healing under a scab so big
he himself mistakenly thought the scab was his skin."

It amused me to hear that some white skin
was healing under my teabark.

I'm not worried about any such disaster as that.
Some slaves were whiter looking than Reverend Dunn; what
healing was taking place there? What about Albino Pearl?

Reverend Dunn looked like a piece of mountain come to life
and he preached from any book, believing that all books,
like everything else, had obtained the Lord's approval to exist
or they wouldn't. According to Reverend Dunn, every word
was God's word, even the foul words which he said were
necessary so the Lord could punish the evil as he couldn't do
with just a dictionary of sorghum.

"Let those who disagree be damned," he said.

That means he'd preach from my book.

from

TOKYO BUTTER

(2006)

Lake Deirdre

On our first trip to Lake Deirdre, *surely it was snowing —only swirls*

as gist remembered: onslaught so relentless, I understand blizzards
                                         —4th of July sparkler iced and flaring
personal comet, hypnotist's wheel, every suggestion cold sunburst

lake acting up, up, uppity —nothing to do with clouds:
its ripples around her toes, my current
orbits

—much like salt, spewed to melt it all: our trips, our Whiskey Island
mine

> *—some are flawless*
> *despite how jewels are extracted, processed*
> *flaunted—*

> *ice cubes melt*
> *into one full glass*

> > > > > > *gargle, gurgle*
> > > > > > *mouth spray, trickle*
> > > > > > *down*

—snow flurries

> *get folded in:*

> *more and more obedience*
> *credo:*
no matter the raggedness of water during storms
later   on ravages repaired without her help,   she just   skated

certain she would not drown
> *solid*
> *landing after lutz, after axel*

every time

I make that happen

                every time:

        more and more obedience

                                I clip unseen wings
                           and there is detritus, snow

                     there is no damage

flat on our backs:
      if we really are angels
the weight of wings
      will pin us down   *proof: sometimes*
          the same as risk:

          we look across lake and see no end
          so cannot speak
          ending the spell of not ending,

          our voices, our words unable   to seem infinite
          not that we require infinity of anything
  —*we require only that lake be big enough to stretch beyond our limits*

                             (one full glass)
                      we required obedience

Inside, snow clinging to me melted quickly, water content
less than that of a tear

yet measurable: trace

          just like permanent transit,
          that I maintain, looped fraction of second

          between falling and arriving

                         —*stay here*

             but I stood by the lake just long enough to wear a snow crown

                                        then walked home with my father
                                where warmer, I was still royal, I was also wet

and Deirdre cried
when I called her   —loyal—   just to tell her that—

          flakes lined up in arcs   *(her eyebrows)*
          row after row   bleached covenants

The Culture of the Missing Song

Cindy Song has been missing since 2001
a new millennium without a trace of butter

—she's now twenty-five, give or take, and likely
employed ethically

based on the sweetness of that face, the pose
chosen from the proof sheet for being sweetest

though she secretly prefers
the one where she looks over her shoulder

with one side of her face framed only by seduction,
the one pose that wouldn't help identify her

in a crowd.

By chance I looked up when her heart-shaped face
was broadcast for less than thirty seconds:

longer looks too risky, as if Cindy were advertising
something, that is not now, just as it wasn't in 2001, for sale,

photo taken when she ranked highly with fellow
graduates, and there was yet no reason
to disappear. She didn't want to be famous

and isn't; after thirty seconds lucky girl is still

in the culture of strangers, occasional handshakes, maybe
she's the one who made my Marriott bed, the sheet fluffed out
a floating landscape, skin of a world

blissful in uniformity of light as it descends
without cliffs or treachery onto the mattress

or she may have been in the back room where taxes
are processed and audits are contemplated, away from
indoor palm and citrus trees of the front office
and reception area, their shadows draping ergonomic chairs

into which her hips, like any, could slide more easily than exotic
tomatoes (tomatillos) and nopales into an unbleached linen bag
that cost twenty dollars and will last a lifetime,

the inked brand circle suggesting a bag of rice, flour, raw
coffee beans or peanuts, a bag right out of the cargo hold
of a ship that cuts into waves, slices crusts of water, and also inches
through the Panama canal,

considered a delicate operation, she's just sitting there
waiting for a gentle dentist, everything rotting so slowly
mistakes are made about what is happening:

sliced crusts of water fold like the skin of a chest
she may have opened to massage a heart just replaced
into beating and continuing a life that will end later, ideally
much later, endless gift of persistent coma

that is an iceberg of hope, cryonic tower
different from a burial vault only in retention of warm
visits, but if she's still meaningfully alive,
as those to whom she is indebted in a variety of ways,
some deeply, have reason to assume,
she has been rude in saying nothing, giving no signs
of the fluctuating status of her health and fortune,

so ungrateful
that perhaps she of all women could be called bitch
without insult or injury or repercussion
beyond, sorry, likely tragic circumstances:

Cindy cut into by schools of barracuda and other aquatic
scavengers so in need of decay, bits of Cindy floating
like scum, coagulates, a floating feast

of risen remains:

flakes as if she came down from heaven
just as family now contends, Cindy fanatics
and fundamentalists, no hour not devoted
to her absence that becomes, by the hour,
more and more a godlike absence

a kind of witness and believer protection program

though more certain is that some Cindy particles
fill the mesh of nets as big as coffee or tomato fields
so the nets come out seeming solid even if empty

as if they've been mended.
Pure speculation.

Accordingly, I can see her in the outline, where it's thickest,
of Comet sprinkled generously—like quicklime
where something died and no other consecration happened—
over the stainless steel of twin sinks, completely covering
and filling in a neat rectangle of *Choregirl* brand sponge,
thicker than an actual fully scaled down gravestone

that allows mowers to pass unchallenged,
shaving the cemetery, keeping wild blooms to a minimum,
only creeping irises, never any vertical morning glory.

I scrub,
provide evidence of religion.

It could be that she delivered mail somewhere,
went to movies, dreamt of cleaner backs of heads
than she ever saw, researched Mata Hari *(Lethrinus nebulosis)*
and defeated a rumor that she resembled an improved Queen
Victoria, then fed a thousand quarters to slot machines
that were in every state and the few reservations
that she visited between serving subpoenas or evictions,
and attaching liens to paychecks and properties
because her job once was to solve delinquencies,

work taken on out of guilt
over her own protracted truancy

during which she became something other than related to
and obligation, the established way that's done:
running away. Driven away. Taken away
by force, at best of her own will: a superlative

so last act of will and power: Cindy
did her best, a ranking usually valid
for only a year, at which time if all else fails

Cindy at home among the homeless:
story of once being a contender, tale of o-my-
how-she-lingers, maybe a Jane Doe ventilator song: endless
fade

of her sweet bone structure:

Cindy Song is a name of a brand of sugar.

::

Next time I'm in Jewell Market, I'll finger boxes
of Jasmine and Basmati rices as a medium would,
last resort at a crime scene

and I really will be weighing something, making
a decision, coming to terms with reality: A hint

of nuttiness, later, in the steam in the kitchen. A love
of almonds. No; a passion. An aardvark tongues

away all steam, restoring a state of blessing
to total erasure.

Heads Wrapped in Flowers

The Easter hats usually exploited gardens
and even when I took mine off, artificial bluebells
were braided into hair

just as they were (white lie)
when Deirdre's son dropped petals
into his mother's casket: one landed
as useless improvement of her mouth.

Years before, Deirdre and I ducked out of service
went to Little Italy's Murray Hill and slurped
things marinara with our decaf to support her crush
on Hill Street Blues' Ed Marinaro who played Coffey

      who wasn't quite the palest thing in her life
      considering what breathed down our necks
      the most inhospitable air they had

      but we had anticipated bad breath,
      we had assumed a garlicky existence

because miracles we then believed in made vampirism
just as plausible. No flowers on the checked-top table

wilted because of atmosphere. From a distance
the beret we saw on a stranger was telling us
walking wounded

and images from former Persian and Ottoman empires
say the same thing, distance failing to be what it was.

We learned Tigris and Euphrates
to help us learn the flowering of existence.

We learned fertile crescent

and we are somehow still amazed

by the fertility of experience: fully-swaddled
babies shaken like perverse maracas   to silence
instead of make the music of rupture persistent:
light bulbs bandaged then fractured under wraps
and again and again those instruments

for crude concerts that parents applauded
with crackle that amplified the filaments' pitiful fizzle:

We didn't have to go much further to love Batman,
Spiderman, Zorro, the Lone Ranger, all masked men
illicitly patronizing convenience

stores

as I do for the implication that merchandise
has been skewed for the expediency of customers:

heads shrunken

and wrapped in price tags, Styrofoam, satin
and certificates of authenticity. Real

old-school prissy passengers

in long-finned convertibles wore nets on their heads
that when wind-whipped became fully bagged

as nets changed position, flimsy umpires appeared
stricken, the net a prototype of shrink-wrap

on these Sunday drives.

The Culture of Saving Cindy's Face

Cindy Song has been missing since 2001
without a trace of butter, lavished instead

with *talc and vapor, moisture from a bath*
that Cathy Song spied, seeing her as Utamaro's *girl*
powdering her neck, where she is still elusive,

faceless, a universal back of head, hair piled
like fan-back chair reserved for company
that doesn't come, hair twisted in relaxed
whiplash curve

like blackened arroyo (her hair a twist of blackened
wicks). There is an ear that doesn't have to be ear
except the logic of its placement, for the lobe is not typical,
the flattened end of a lever that begins just under the chair,
that if lifted would also raise the chair, perhaps freeing
small birds though, if there, they've been at ease nesting
in the head, enjoying free range of wider shoulders
where wingspan became possible. Stone-faced, equally

at home in gardens that old cemeteries become whether or not left
alone, stone girls on pedestals, cracked wings shedding pebbles,
studding the ground with fossilized eyes. Possible source
of the powder with which she powders her neck, adds
substance; she is delaying decay as avalanche. I am also stalling

so as not to have to deal with the lack of face. If not respect,
it could be shyness, demure approach usually successful
that is at work, but I doubt it, since embarrassment or despair
about facelessness would supercede a classically feminine
approach. There was a need to classify

such births as ordinary for the Andaman Islands
with a falsely documented evolution that parallels genuine
independent evolutions in Madagascar. John Mandeville

had revelations of the gloriously grotesque: a precedent
established by John the Divine on Patmos,
so discrediting Mandeville for not having voyaged literally
doesn't wash, and arguably his small habit of hallucinogens
self-prescribed to fortify his weak constitution
was a vehicle which did transport him. More accepted

is an account of such a no-face birth in the fifteenth century
to a woman from whom such deformity was expected,
she'd been accused of every known sin,
and some secretly admired her (I assume) for creating new ones,
wondering what it might mean if her talent could be diverted
to the good, falling short of calling this diversion salvation.

The child didn't live
long, and the facial plane wasn't flat, but none of the features
fully popped out, as if they were retractable, and had retreated
into little bunkers.

To get at the mouth behind nonexistent lips
required pokes and surgical travels not then perfected; the cry,
some say the baby did cry, and left the midwife dead (the first honest
stab at cry—it really did pierce) was as from a well the baby
had fallen into, the face indeed seemed to have fallen, a typical
first-soufflé face, eyes presumably could look at their own
orbital sockets and see some of the brain
as a cave of mammillated stalactites

though the baby, considered unfortunate and condemned,
born this way to emphasize lack of innocence and humanity
(which the lack of innocence should have confirmed),
the undescended testes no help in proving anything useful
to a case for consecrated burial, had no language,
nor did anyone else, for this condition
that was thought to be devoid of human condition,

given the thin evidence of forked tail insemination:
The skin that buried the face

though thin was more elastic than usual, a stretch
not prone to rupture yet more delicate than nylon stockings,
so it was easy to poke most anything through, a fatal
fingernail of failed midwifery right through that face
sealed in opalescence associated also with angels
though none had been captured for examination, and at
that point, there were not any more advanced alien studies

so the mother, though no one actually called her that,
couldn't claim forced copulation
with voyagers coming to earth to plant their seeds
—and where better than inside so much ego,
when relative fertility is compared? Also, better to resist

comparison that might have had some validity, realized
those too aware that Mary herself had given birth to something
that exceeded humanity, no gospel writers emphasizing
His normality
but rather how divinity manifested itself—even so, He did
resemble Mary, that's who everybody said He looked like.
This faceless child of Germany in truth perhaps better resembled
the facelessness of God who doesn't see with human eyes
or hear with human ears, & so forth, exceeding limits
of human sensing way more than bees, bats, dogs more on
His level of perception. That the exceptional child

did not live long was good, and perhaps arranged:
a smothering
although facial features were already smothered
by skin that already covered it like a sheet pulled
to cover up the dead with a less offensive muslin
easier on the narrow range of human sight.
It may have breathed, this strange boy whose name

was withheld for fear of cursing any other Hans.
Strange Boy
seemed name enough. But to call Utamaro's girl a victim

of facelessness isn't quite right; it seems she'd need just to turn
to show her face, except that it's detached, lays on the mirror
the faceless girl holds at an angle that could not catch
her own reflection, so the mirror's face comes from elsewhere
and the faceless girl looks beyond it:
the mirror is aimed over her shoulder,
the face in it is there as something on a platter, as a cameo
for a giant, whitened lily on a reflective pool without current,
without need for anchors, not far enough out
to have to look for harbor that should not be the default position,
and what's on the platter looks like Cindy Song, exactly

the way that I remember Cindy Song, missing since 2001,
as Utamaro divined she would be when he painted her face
and only her face in the eighteenth century, finding
what a girl would lose in the nineteen-eighties when born faceless
to a more resourceful family, the luck of existing

when there's more skill in exploiting resources, in taking
advantage of both medical and mystical advances,
so her parents lifted the face
from the painted girl who offered it to anyone in the future
who might know how to make a face stick, take vein and root
in the rich soil and dirt of evolved flesh, and become real:

Utamaro's girl did have a mask
that Cathy Song found irresistible, its extension
into a *curve of shoulder like the slope of a hill*
set deep in snow
in a country of huge white solemn birds.

At the end of 2003 I saw that face again detached:
a photo of Cindy that was all face, as if lifted again
from the reflective platter thousands of atoms away
from a neck being powdered into existence,
and I'm not going to find Cindy with that face

that she has taken off, that flower whose wilt
she has discarded, unable to put it back on
after stepping out of her bath so refreshed,
like somebody else, the molt behind her reaching
the drain.

Postscript Culture of Head Wraps

Her knuckles exasperated, my aunt as dead as Deirdre
cried for a washboard: it had been too long
since the last scrub's knuckle-peel

through which she gauged conversion: responses
to the fear of bleach to which she'd become immune

so did not whiten, did not use it to fake vitiligo, did not surpass
her rest home cook's uniform like her sister Maid's and sister LPN's

all beaten by Black Muslim women on Superior Avenue
where we were too, without the centerpiece

that makes a difference, especially since it sits atop
Black Muslim female heads like a linen pyramid or
sphinx.   The riddle of faith in stitches.

Her knuckles exasperated, my hand squeezed
into its own exasperation, we walked through

all that Muslim whitewater on Superior, through all that white-
capped spun flax sea of hospitality and urgency of nurses

everywhere, superior treatment of that location, though
whiteheads are also pimple eruption when sebaceous glands

are blocked—I've always been stuck with dualities,
wasn't pulled into the sea that could have claimed, that must
have parted as women aren't navigable
unless they move or are moved, and I was no force, still

am not ready to wrestle with *Soft as Silk* and *Swan's Down*
cake flour, boxes of contenders ten years in the cupboard

waiting for promised attempt at scratch, probably full of pontoons,
webs of temporary ropes in the ring, towel thrown over the head

to let dough rest, just to be let near sanctuary, to blend in
with immaculate covering of civil unrest in facilities of praise,
white head wraps kicking back

any light hitting them, these white heads also frosted
bay windows, conspicuous on the street, a recess

inside where the personal sits; if allowed
to happen, the cake can still be cake, the rise

not necessarily compromised if webbed flour
turns out layers of lace, a more patterned cake,

structure less that of foam, more that of washboard
also present in magnification of linen's tight white weave.

Victim of the Culture of Facelessness

To call Utamaro's girl a victim
of facelessness isn't quite right

because of what depleted uranium is doing
to babies in what used to be Babylon; it isn't quite right
to call some of the variations faces

because the markers aren't there, the noses,
the eyes, the mouths—what face without them?
what irony—though it isn't quite enough

to call it ironic—that when faces may be uncovered,
cauls and veils slowly lifted, there is nothing
underneath some of them but blankness

as if cauls and veils had been erasers. To call it
clean slate and fresh start isn't quite right.
That there is voicelessness goes without saying,
will have to go without saying

though other parts of the body can produce sound,
especially offensive noises as if to express dissatisfaction,
normality, disgust. Legal documents can still

be signed as blindly as ever, attorneys will still have power
and will still be below the threshold for determining
what is absolute. International frogs

are sympathizers, the odd-numbered legs,
even-numbered heads; the frogs quietly take on
entanglement, linked to consequences

of what is done to infants no matter how well isolated
these events are to certain cities and beliefs. Particles
leak. Every day, more

codes to break, to access codes intact under them,
Paul Tessier a good example, his smashing of cadaver skulls
against stone walls, some blocks already stained enough
with grapes and white peaches
though those peche blanc stains were invisible,
but he sensed them, so smashed
skulls there, in locations accustomed to upheaval
on many scales, blind moths flew into them

and made a splash of wing like paint
—not every night, but often enough—
and Tessier broke the code by breaking skulls
to learn the pattern of cranial and facial breakage,
the preferences of fracture,

and then the motivation to learn how to reset bones, tiny pieces
as delicate as picking the delectable from escargot
whose shells Tessier could crush in his hand, and did,
to overcome his patience, his idea
about skull fracture entangled with how he ate snails,
how his vocal cords expanded in a culture of red wine
just as mind should expand; entanglement can deform
and reform but doesn't have to. And yet

twin Muscovites reportedly born this millennium
have been affected, one born with no face, the other
born with two, reputable physicians
would have the world believe, and the obvious,
which has been a part of none of this,
so can mix with nothing, is not a consideration;

the extra face can be removed and transferred, but there
is hesitation in the name of preservation
of once-in-a-millennium occurrence not mistaken
for second coming despite the timing. The faces are layered,
the same blood vessels route through both, loop dependency:

they are his nourished personality, they already help
him dig deeper:
                        the deeper face faces inward,
though the stack, not being aligned perfectly,
allows one eye to see behind him peripherally.
He is making money already, a medical first,
still called medical impossibility, a moral first
for the genuine literality of two-facedness.

A fee to see him, study him, figure out
how to burp him, to see for yourself if he vomits
from both mouths. A fee that helps his brother
whose life is easier, pampered, because there is nothing
to see, to pick out his face from the crowd,
it is necessary to look at the doubled brother.

It is hard to say which products might be right for him
to endorse, which sales might double
because I have sympathy. He can not give up any of this
to the twin born without complexity,
eating through a tube just as insects do
sucking up nectar
that could all come from the flowers in the room;
his toes twitch as if he smells them. Face parts
or whole face collected from the generous dead

can somehow be attached or combined
with conventional prosthetics; he has an optic
nerve, olfactory and auditory canals, set
of drums, plumbing, the underground
rigging, the pipes, shallow roots of milk teeth, two
shallow holes (as if vampires assisted) doing
the nose's job so that he breathes, airway is there,
everything that should be below the surface is. Growing

up by Chernobyl, his mom loved the passage
of geese. In general loved examples of flight.
She looked for this.
Hundreds of birds could come together to make solid
night sky, separating after many hours to allow light
by reducing and minimizing wings. As if just for her,
perhaps the only one watching. Nuclear waste
flew one day into her soup, and that was that, fallopian
and ovarian hocus pocus and harem scarem, that old
black magic putting on another show. Too many nuked cooks
spoil her broth, so many molecules, billions and billions
of atoms serving her air and everything: try to tip them all.

Even if this is a hoax, it serves some need someone has
to test believability, and to test balance. There is some need
to fabricate it and accept whatever comes because no one knows
the limits of what can come, because in everything is some
necessity: that is the cruelty of jokes and of imagination.

The boys were cheek to cheek in utero, there was a bond;
they couldn't overcome it, when they had to separate
to be born individually, one face came off, sticking
to his brother, stamps do that, that brother keeping
his brother's face, entangled, desperate love

—like divers sharing a tank of oxygen, I want to think,
because that is beautiful, their heads together,
their unity of four kicking legs, their joint bubbles
like fertilized eggs surrounding an octopus
becoming a small cathedral.

Ghee Glee

Each churn sculpts butter differently, marks it
not exactly as a gun barrel marks its projectile
but churning and firing the revolver have more in common
than that which doesn't mark or isn't marked.
I am relieved to know that effort encrypts

that goat's milk soap soothes, goat cheese and butter
combat genetic sensitivities, and like any other combat

offer mixed results

that vary more widely after the freshness date, the best-if-
bought-by stamp. Nostalgia is not exempt, becomes more
and more decadent as time advances: good old turbulent
familiar decades

are historical for children who have nuclear tests also,
ground wars over seas just as rough. Books seem benign
no matter what seethes
behind words the mind can attach emotion to: ink
just bleeds, and pages supposedly inflammatory,
sometimes banned, feel so smooth; more and more
of them are acid-free:

Butter. Pure butter. No need to limit what is only said
thought   dreamed: partial realities that melt like butter.
I feel so fortunate to be part putty: amoeboid butter
engulfing what I encounter, complex destiny because of complex
identity: I am never completely out of place
(many choices for where to shelve this book, each a best choice)

and my presence   which must be dealt with   gets churned into
the meaning of what occurs there.
Assumptions butter the mind   or coat it so that
what it doesn't want can't easily get through: butter barrier
greased pig thinking   but once on your skin

butter can feel like your own secretion, your own rich oil:
bounty ooze   crown melt   —if only there was only toast

in the picture, deli buns, biscuits, croissants, beignets
more obvious reasons to lay it on thickly, but sticks of butter
come architect-ready to build a house, plantation columns
and nothing is easier to sculpt
than pale butter skin all the way through, bone-free, dull knives
glide renewed,   resuscitated: ghee glee. Even some tigers
take on the purity of butter
when sunbeams melt on them   like a web, snare of light

                                        solar churn

                        toasty equatorial residents

but I don't take croissants with butter other than
what batter subsumes,   internalizes
deprivation also appeals, demands of heritage
(I don't deny all of them
or any of them in expected ways) hardtack homage, pilot bread, ship
biscuit, going to and from difficult places, some in, some out of my league
especially if visited
at the time of day that all shadows are gaunt, as if at least

one parent
is a butter knife: the father

is the usual suspect, related assumptions implicated him
in Cindy's disappearance in 2001 without a trace of butter,
maybe this very butter, withering from the sides of the container
                                        slick with
what was lost to surface. For maximum fun with butter,
that part of legacy (my father an unsalted butter-color man):

a fresh tub for each impression. One for chin, one for hand, another
for foot, each bite mark.   No problem: there was always
another butter. Exceptional mortar butter, plaster of butter
                                                                    every year
Easter butter lamb to butcher gently with polite knives
the shape of oars, shape of skinny hooded priest profiles.

You stuck your hands in, the butter softened cuticles, repaired
dishpan hands, soothed scrapes, minor burns —Mama ran   butter-fisted
when I fell off the bike—   was elbow grease
if you wiped it there, and let rings come off as if it was before:
                                                                    softness back
and some of your innocence

in family tradition of Blue Bonnet, Mazola, Land o' Lakes'
Indian maiden coming at me sometimes in a canoe taken as rescue

craft I was too big for; I could open my mouth, and she, Princess
Whatchamacallher could float right in, down

my throat that with tonsils and tongue offered a take
on southwestern land formations. We used Big Chief
baking powder and sugar, had Minnehaha Water delivered

in jugs big enough to have held fleets of sunken toy ships,
and sold what we called bog water (taken from vases
and saucers under potted plants, spruced up
with Listerine) to those who wanted adult drinks prematurely;
                                                            —¡O Deirdre!—
bog water of premature wine not done fermenting had to be
priced by proximity to process completion. After any of this
we freshened the air with Indian Blessing Spray #41

that stank a little bit
and also smelled a little bit like cherries. By not

partaking of any butter, not indulging, not giving in
my toast was sandpaper, the usual slice of fossil-sponge
Martian terrain close-up. But it could crumble, could
become dust in my fingertips, could look as if I crumbled
with it, tobacco like, filler for my father's Pall Malls
that he smoked to death, and as if I were butter
—had that responsibility   time to time   I opened cigarettes
scraped the paper clean   and wrote haiku riddles that I rolled up
tightly,   my words burning from his lips   easily

gone gone   gone

All four slices of my wooden bread
are sanded smooth grain.   *Old English*
protected   —that oil like supremely clarified butter.
What fine head and foot boards   for beautiful small beds
no one fits, only if the size of cigarettes, pack of white-robed sisters
from Virginia   what fine understated tombstones.
This bread may be waxed. O shine. I know who Shine was.
Its lines are durable labyrinths   *our father*

fingers and tongue may follow in cursive spell-out.
That wax, that sheen of get-away

from the path shines my fingerprints
where I grip the bread as loose pages, loose leaves
of suspicious adaptation. Loops under the arches
are a green onion bulb
cross section, innermost loop

like the eye of an embroidery needle
or like sperm-head
or like the hook
that scrapes out early pregnancy

depending on who's looking. The loop made
when tying the ribbons of a blue bonnet

under the chin.

The Subculture of the Wrongfully Accused

Ultimately improved by it: slant light
hitting his prison obliquely

near the state bird's pointed head   accentuated
crest, the black-ringed bill

from which *wheat-wheat-wheat-*   *wheat*
from which *whoit cheer, whoit cheer;*   *cheer-*
cheer-cheer

inspired Ronald Cotton to listen
as in his head, the solitary cardinal   indulged in snails

which seemed like polished fossils
of trophy hog tails   (after prize   butchery)

that Ronald was able to recall,
his hair a mess of replicas of them

as industrious as the state
whose success was poultry & eggs   tobacco & soybeans

as well as convictions:

None as tightly knit as Jennifer's   (not even the state flag)
that she could identify Cotton

that cotton's taking on appearances   other than burst white
of a dense localized haze from which to weave memory, following
pink-petaled start, rather a satellite   dish of a flower, pollen/sensor-
studded antenna protruding from   the center

undeniably; the jury couldn't acquit   Cotton
of its role in documenting and altering   Jennifer's history,

many lives changed

as result of consequences, sensors   that boast duality
of receptor and transmitter: witness: insects give and take, taint
what is put out, taken in; mix
it up so that interrelatedness   spreads
and the understandable error of   metaphor
becomes less erroneous over time:
eleven years in prison, innocence   locked up, protected

although in prison, it resembled   something else.
If Cotton strained, he could see   the top

of a Ferris wheel on the horizon   just a possible
segment of a rainbow the length   of a chain

of cardinal feathers

even though it wasn't that at all.   The eye witnesses all the time,
even the unseeing eye is turned   toward a focus
on black, saturation dense as   conviction; the eye

processes, pulls in whole vista to a   retinal speck
of convergence

which is to say there is some Cotton   in Poole,
some connection, independent   shared participation in cold
beer, occasional cards turkey-spread
in the right hand without knowing   the other
sank into the seat at the cinema   the same way

and sampled Funnel cake at the   state fair
within a week of each other

and more than that in common: both being men
and convicted for what men really can and really do, do.

Including sometimes confessions   and apologies; cash reparations

176

after the innocence is free to extend its parameters
to unlocked doors, be an oversized   over-zealous white bird
floating down the aisle, its cottony   haze lifted
in order to kiss and marry Ronald's   calm delight in being able
to take his time

leave his longshoreman's mark on   ships
that take some of him to any port in the world: durable goods

such as the DNA whose precision   detects human exactitude,
and could build as many Ronalds as   time would permit

something Jennifer now desperately   wants to do, restoring
what was lost because it was like   something else,

because the fact of similarity   is compelling, convincing;
if connections could not be made,   there'd be no havens, no fugitive
status lost to fusion, no links   to God, no human

murmurings whose   constant echoes
are also the gentle silvery hum   of fans praying
over computer motors to cool them   and also mimic
motion of small wings amplified   to make sound

in the distance much like   the electric razor
preparing a head on death row   clean as a light bulb.

Ronald was prepared to be believed;
he saw the quiet manner of his long days in court
as evidence of his rationality and   contemplativeness

such as befits clergy; a potential   propensity for order,
mercy, the steadiness required to   dispense blessings
mostly on the undeserving without   emotion or judgment
selfishness or preference

while he was being judged guilty for   lack of emotion,
for Jennifer's incontrovertible emotional insistence
on Cotton's being the one—she had   to finger him
to be comfortable within her survival.   No way to mistake
to ever forget details documented in   memory,
the event relived to the point that it   resculpted her brain
into a Cottony bust (he was there   to be the perfect model)

whose reality floated away   in a Poole,
as only the reflection of Cotton

identified as source. A situation   also called (must-have) moonlight.

Here's the new & improved Cotton: eleven years in the making; enough
time served to anger to ruin it; at that   same room's temperature
it became doubt of clemency, pardon: peculiar butter that erupted
as gratefulness for the miracle of absolute exoneration
when his impossibility as rapist   was proven.

Even Cotton conceded that   the composite sketch
bore a just resemblance to Cotton,   displayed a metaphor for men
like Cotton, the seeds of capability   in the structure of the face,
the human repertoire that includes   Cotton
who softly consents to meet Jennifer when she asks him to
funnel her regret and apologies deep into himself, accepting that
she meant no malice toward him   but toward
the perpetrator whom many men   resemble, all
brothers, family

of man resemblance; Cotton's   own daughter, Cotton's own wife
could be in a similar position; no   offense
taken, captivated by the beauty of   Jennifer; her superior logic

refusing to let the crime against her
silence her; as sure, as certain, as   dazzling
about speaking up about mistaking   Cotton for Poole

as she was in identifying   in the lineup
the closest thing there to Poole   the best
available, the incredible   likeness
that memory seized, filling gaps in   the recollected Poole
with Cotton's particulars.   She felt better in her cotton-touched skin.

Metaphor is a form of forgiveness; a short rope of it knots-up
those that can't come together any other way into being defined
by the other. Strange

and estranged pairings give rise to mutable truth
that can yield to both dawn and twilight
demands that things be seen differently.

Jennifer in moonlight instead of being illuminated moon whose face
was also in Emmett Till's way, but this generation of Jennifer has another side
home late after a day of good faith   in which she and Cotton team up
at a church to speak up about doubt as less a shadow than certainty.

Memory is as accurate as metaphor, an overlay
that always fits something, that like the purest
most sparkling water is too naïve   not to submit
to any vessel into which it's poured.   Just to be guzzled.

Perhaps the vessel in which cotton   becomes a pool
in which North Carolina is shaped   like an embryo:

Humanity still on the brink   of infancy.

The Unbuttered Subculture of Cindy Birdsong

Of course, there are obvious, frankly, reasons that the missing
Cindy Song (since 2001) brings Cindy Birdsong to mind, another

disappearance from my life, though even when she was active
—overly generous—in my entertained days, she was replacement

for a missing Supreme after Diana and then Florence
departed, and after there was some flap really important

to those flapping but hardly worth resurrecting
seeing as she can still sing like an unspecified backup bird,

so no surprise that she's just an afterthought
here because of Cindy Song who can't be here
though CB sometimes took the lead in pop tunes

nobody talks about much unless necessary in trivial games
where stakes can be lucrative, millionaires made

for knowing Cindy Birdsong was a Supreme, as little
as that, though at the very least she was also a daughter

and was probably at least once somebody's lover
and perhaps the recipient of fan mail and hate mail

because she was a Supreme, after being a Bluebelle
at just about the time that there were still Queens for a Day,

though rarely African Queens on that game show, all the royalty
proud recipients of new Frigidaires, Amanas, Bissells, & Hoovers.

Cindy's certainly not the only afterthought; the linen bag
of tomatillos not far from here is another, the shape appealing
in the challenged corner of my eye, contorted as if everything's
taken in the gut; in one version it has a drawstring

that can be pulled noose-tight
then gets turned upside down
into ideal bag over
shrunken head about to be hung
though shrunken heads don't need redundant trip
to the gallows

especially since they usually travel better, to non-publicized
auctions as they make their way into collections. The Jivaro
of Ecuador made them best, *tsantas,* skull-less heads
rather like hairy dates and dried plums, a kind of rum cake
with lips stitched, a kind of sturdy yarn cup. The majority

of shrunken heads I've seen have shar-pei faces
or something that's found in the dark

center when a radiation-altered sunflower head opens,

though this majority needs to be qualified,
as I've seen only a half dozen shrunken heads

outside of movies
and most of those were monkey heads (mostly in Toronto)
though they weren't saying only monkey, resemblances
& so forth, though covering up and burial aren't necessarily
more respectable than trophies

unless the corpse proves incorruptible and becomes patron
saint of compact embalming—not that, though it could be,
the goodness of John the Baptist is shrinkable. Mostly

thinking must be revised: like many, I once thought everything
on television was in television, shrunken to fit into the box

in which case Cindy Birdsong would have been the most
remarkable of the shrunken heads, singing up a storm

the way she did the last time I saw her
& loved her in color that could be changed,
at volumes that could be changed

but she could not be enlarged
without getting out of the box

of static and cathode rays, streaming
electrons, without giving up

hordes of atomic
and subatomic groupies.

The Partial Mummy of Head Wrap Extension

gets in the Crimean War, with the bandages
on the little princess's father's amnesiac head

as tonic against damage underneath,
sterile tonic against infection:

       Florence Nightingale's system
       of circulating antisepsis.

I see that wrapped dome
and then I can see the Capital

and the political in all landscapes,
snow wrapping the head of the Himalayas
while flowers thousands of feet below
blossom into feet

that seem to be bathing in gardens; insects
swarm the equivalent of rain

after I see the wrapped amnesiac dome,
plaster cast of a fruit bowl
as if the sick man tries on breakfast.

       Fathers sometimes falter.

       Some fathers say they want to falter,
       they are wrapped up

       in y-chromosomes threatened
       with extinction. Their policy.

       Deirdre is not upset, she's put her mark,
       an X on her son to compensate for her loss

of husband, his Y both excuse and reason;
Y-not?

The male defining chromosome was previously thought of
as a wasteland where genes go to die.
There is a needed, Deirdre will also tell you, *quest*
to bring respectability to the Y

The Y naturally seeks itself, wraps itself in itself
as if, Y's logic, to cut back on mutation.

What chromosomes do, does not sound respectable:
no men are moral at the molecular level.

—Perhaps some wear the weight of that on their heads.

Pairs of chromosomes swap genes to complicate things
for mutation, to foil some elementary paternity,

but the Y is stag, and swaps with itself,
self-same sequencing, just reversed as in a mirror,

up and down the double helix streets, a do-wop group
on every corner, looking good, sometimes veering off-key

and mutating themselves out of a sperm dance
to go with the *please Baby, please Deirdre* song.

Because it has to, why else? *every man's Y contains*
600 DNA letters that differ from his father's,

and there are fifty million letters in Y's finished sequence.
Y mutates, perseveres, and becomes infertile

thousands of times more than the normal mutation rate,
almost making it possible to understand why Deirdre's
mutant Jerome was so unfaithful and insolvent. He had 600
additional ways to twist the alphabet of his promises

yet he failed seventh grade math, Miss Barufaldi's class, the grading
on a curve.

He wrapped Deirdre in regret. He brought her battle
in bed,   didn't butter her up
and she didn't bring it up   except to explain
choices she didn't forget she had

until she died, and as far as I can tell, then promptly

forgot everything even that

The Blue Men of the Sahara are often also
better men
picking up tint from what they wear, what
they are seen in: their revelatory traffic
of behavior

in which so much is risked, so they wrap
their orifices against evil and dust storms
and the relocation efforts of grit

and vault their thoughts in turbans.

It must be easier,

under the *obmubilatio capitis,* under the imposition
of the veil

under the turbans and wraps
of luxurious moral and chromatic color

to let a peony span the mind, to become
a flower at home in a garden of exoneration:

a little bliss-head   with a pistil and a stigma.

Deirdre: A Search Engine *(excerpt)*

She went to Italy

        and then she died

                a woman with her,
                that none of the living-
                without-her
                knew, had bangs:

overwhelming sight   limp fevered petals
of bathers, & sail   why not?   gathered into barrettes
              left was only caves   like hair

viewed at the impossible angle
of things without noticeable end   hers
also no finale   was dark water
          mud flaps of the big rigs   stiffened, sealess,

                    fishless; just hair,
         for cover   fine, flexible protein
                    strings

not unknown to clouds
the side of it a thin line,
a cut
         her ex-husband's laundry   paltry with shreds
that from distance   where he left it   and rags of atmosphere
is horizon and necessary   folded like cliffs
to purpose   leg holes of his briefs   virga over Patmos
                like craters
she laid figs on her lips   whose lost substance   like something smug
                and credibility
                became moons   without reason

in the Presence of Mourners.

Every toadstool was uprooted.
Neighbor children's fingers were so fat
each would grow into a pig.
There was that much faith—wasn't it that?
in moonlight

that filled buckets during one session of pleading with it
to give and yield and fill

　　　Deirdre—

What is it for, this reflection? Delight?
Everything can't be for that?

Twist, shimmy, worm into it, force

a delighted huddle

　　　　a fence of crooked spines, guardian nurses
　　　　as the children, retarded, sniffling, rubbing bottoms
　　　　of their noses, a finger of pig
　　　　curved like an extension of upper lip
　　　　poked out like a roof over shingles of teeth
　　　　white as nothing, those teeth pure exception

pulled up the toadstools

that looked so much like nails
and needed so much to be hammered
into something, but up against those teeth of pure exception?

Later that day: open house, the realtor
showing it to strangers:

Deirdre's house

yet there were no strangers to compromise loss, everyone's in
a related stage of grief or recovery, choosing to look at it that way,
unable to look at it without a way to perceive

moonlight   (7 April)

in fog sweeping over the bay
where seven were killed in a planned boating accident,
motors cutting flesh in the way of a machine's priorities,
skin like colonies of plankton and baby seastars, baby jellies
and seahorses as transparent as innocence can be conceived,

on the surface, where the skin was used to being
part of the water's shimmer
that Deirdre's fingers disrupted
to make circles as tight as the curl of her hair
in the Italian humidity that everyone else raved about

huddled around ruins.

(Gloria's lilies)

Deirdre lived beyond that lawn
as green as any lawn had ever been,

when green became necessary
in order to bear

the conviction coming clear   (his own testimony)
in her husband, whose charm had been a scam fortune
earned in espionage, sanctioned marauding until
his orders came through as an astronaut, only till then.

                                                  (faithful Deirdre, at the

mailbox

                                        everyday, country-style,
                                        on a stick by the dirt road,

wild

                                        lilies wilder there than
                                        on any other part of the

property,

                                        vining up the stick, into the

box,

                                        postcards with pistils and

petals,

                                        no return address, on Easter
Sunday   more anonymous flowers)

        And then Easy Street, really in her town, a cul-de-sac
        where families rode bicycles and ate sandwiches in & below
anonymous trees,
        and meant to have more of those moments, and tried not to
blame
        each other for successes or failures, for the obvious reason
        of misinterpretation, the quietest moments occurring
        between men and women married, but not to each other
        though it did prove that seeds didn't really care where
        they were planted, a flower would be flower wherever
        it grew Buttercup, Daisy, Crazy Phlox and Peony,
deadly
        ricin in the castor plant that has a habit of flowering,
Nerium
        oleander, rosebay, wolfsbane wild and cultivated,

        it's settled:

his orbit was to be her engagement and wedding
rings, but she'd have to do the actual traveling in
neglected circles.

His baby was how she found equator

of her ample middle
her plum of forgiveness

that moved during the wedding as if her unborn son
was in love, the enticing vow wowing him, *cleave* and *cherish*

whose syllables were part of babytalk.
Mother and son stayed close

when bombs fell

on schedule everywhere that they were falling

the little bombs, vials, ampules
cracking open in gas chambers and in veins, traveling
in her estranged husband's truly blue ones (but no truth serum).
color of guilt, rainbow of guilt
as her water broke
         along with old records.

        He was the only man she knew not impressed by rivers.

Was it a cool drip into his arm? Can there be dependence
on sodium pentothal? Did he feel that shrunken submarine?
every torpedo of what he considered relief? Did he imagine impact
of one more dream coming as true as truth could be to someone
who didn't socialize on that level of bluntness

where things got fat and ugly (especially a good third trimester)

just as decaying mirages did, wide oases, broad
palm leaves misplaced being at the tops of trees
where they suggested mature women's hips
despite where they were

just as there was always weather

in which it was safe to fly a kite: go ahead,
nothing's there but electricity, the secret of light,

he urged, her birthday forgotten, be a kid again, paid a kid
five dollars for his kite struggling in Woodhill Park, gave her magic

of a silk scarf from around his neck (office gift to him, secret
Santa) (the only one from which he pulled, eked
out everything else he gave her) to be the kite's tail, the secret
of maintaining flight. He was not exempt
from horizon, was himself the vanishing point:
some kind of kooky convergence
of implications of everything
with evidence of nothing, source
of redemption for a few definitions.

Deirdre's man was a good man   (or she wouldn't have become
involved; she called him *Sweet Jerome* for a reason); it was good of him

to get it off the ground: kite, coffin, virginity;
a full carat crystal of quartz in which so much is blurred
when slipped on a finger to complete
a second, third, fourth proposal
each followed by ceremony. Bought the largest ring he could
so it circles the finger and needs adjustment—*uh-oh!* see
his wad of bills for what the jeweler loses, *sorry, Baby; blessed insurance*
—the heck with getting another just-a-symbol; Deirdre already felt like
a one and only;   the only one to endure this:

                                  the diamond cutter
                                  and fire eater
                                  lived out their natural lives together
                                  Her fingernails were overtly
            porous.
                                  Molecular gaps
                                  for some reason
that didn't matter to science
                                  so science left it alone. Left to their own
            devices
                                  each nail was a slice of bread, full of
physics of foam,   (despite emancipation)
                                  really soaked up olive oil and balsamic
concoctions   especially
                                  since that was what they were most
frequently in:

                                  Because bread was part of her, there were
severe implications   for her bones: French bread arms,
challah thighs   and she didn't want
                                  to lose that the way she'd already lost
                                  a dozen angels
(baby cakes)   (little Debbies)   (Ho-Ho's)   (Anita Baker CDs)
                                  and custard cups, as if those were related
                                  losses, the quantifiable
                                  and the unquantifiable right next to it:
            do-it-yourself clones.   Boxed set.
                                  Dragonflies picked the fire eater's
                                  nose, the singing made the secretions
            buttery in the mind
                                  of the fire eater, and that was therefore
            the scent given off,
                                  something the dragonflies in this vista
            adapted to.
                                  A dynamic system. Everything pitched in.
            Pinched. The waist cincher really pleased him.

Crimped. A hallelujah every now
and then, but it was called many things,
the effect didn't change, on and on.

She sucked the oil out of her fingernails
and bit them,
oil-softened sucked toast, old wheat.

He didn't complain, for his palms had evidence
of old irrigation systems that had sponsored wheat.

Sometimes they rented a catamaran

from a jewel thief and smuggler

because they had to take care of each other

and they could forgive the occasional brawls,
fistfights, because those came with
the compensation
of flowers that grew as tangled as anything else
when left alone to decide what growth was: where,
how, why

blossoming is such a good thing, a fist opening, closing
pumps the blood
circulates fragrance: look out now! insects & their
inspiring public quickies,
botanical promiscuity: her husband bee a man

—Do you understand why Deirdre threw them down,
why she plucked the arches over her eyes free of
skinny petals
careful to uproot the follicular seed? She wasn't about to grow
any trifling clones of thorns

194

> but everything blossomed, opened, swelled

to the point of exposure, revelation; she didn't see it coming,
but it got there: a way to get in, gnaw, peck, excavate, unfurl magnificently;
think: *onion, onion,* skin coming off in layer upon layer of radiation sickness,
long-finger white radish prosthetic ingenuity blossoming in desperation
to make the music of this meaningful by transcending its plain truth: radishes
wet-noodle tied to knuckles, and these radish out the scales and chords,
the garden sings and there is rapture

and Deirdre is a bride

and is buried in something even whiter:

the uniform of Eastern Star mysticism
that meant nothing to her before she died
because she went to Italy
when it wasn't safe:

no reliable beliefs in her pocket   of nail crumbs.

Everything about her dead says Order of Eastern Star,
and by order, everything is tightlipped, silent, under
the rigmarole, autopsy because she was supposed to recover.

Biggest flower of life was an aneurysm in her brain
still collegiate when she's turning fifty
whether or not she's ready, treating herself to Italy, a villa as if
that's what it's all about: hills that won't be shy there, one shoulder cozy &
familiar with another, tessellating on every possible plane and the space
between them, tessellated time, no gaps, but maybe not the fill of choice, free
will and chaos all chucking out symmetry, overriding and entangling similarity
in which to plug undesirable and desirable details, inspiring and uninspiring
specificity: which is which? If it touches Deirdre, it's relevant.
Building blocks.

NEW POEMS

(2016)

Hypnosis at the Bird Factory

(there is)

A parade of accidents.
A war is over
so a smokestack chokes

(indicating presence of)

an unstable reservoir of pressure

(that)

forces relief: a release
of manufactured birds

(upon release)

dark density flies

(these releases are also
outbreaks; released, they become)

winged epidemics

(which when slightly magnified,
are revealed to be, on this magnified scale)

festivals of beaks

(easily connected to)

synchronized hungers

(that)

feed little avian shops of horrors

                                        (that)

feed little avian shops of delight

                                (shifting the gaze to other angles
                                available from the observer's location,
                                it is possible to notice)

a similar address of leaf storm feathers

                                (part of which is Gabriel Garcia
                        Marquez' short story, "Leaf Storm," as
                the title of the novella is usually
            translated in English, yet something
        else, in all likelihood, when translated
    into other languages from an English
    translation and not directly from the
                                Spanish, which is a translation anyway,
                                of an idea and all of its components, a
                                translation very much a form of
                transformation, allowing what is called
        magical realism to be a factual
accounting system of empirical and
aesthetic events, imagination available
to process any empirical evidence.
                        This phrase: *leaf storm feathers,*
                    examined before extending the
            consideration to include what follows the
            phrase, **is able to** [more easily]
    function, as either or both compound
        noun and compound   **verb**
    system, as either function is   **consistent**
    with easy-to-construct   **literal**
        understandings   [though these
literalities may be   experienced only in the

200

mind] **of**

of

behavior of [likely a group or pile

leaves so as to simultaneously

construct a context in which both *leaf*

and *storm* contribute to the group

identity of the phrase, as evidenced by

the use of *address* to denote a form of

shared occupancy. As a contextual

community modified by a shared

practice of limiting [and extending]

what is possible for group meanings

that contain only what can be

constructed that intersects all three.

The leaf storm *feathers*;

something happens to the leaf storm

associated with properties of feather.

Or the feathers being considered are

of a variety associated with leaf

storms, *leaf-storm* feathers,

distinguishable from other feather

types.

On some scale, *leaf storm feathers*

easily encourages mental constructions

of raggedness, uneven edges easily

associated with feathers which

resemble, in this language grouping,

the system of veins in a generalized

understanding of leaf structure. Some

form of storm [weather system or insect

system—such as locust swarm—for

instance] may have damaged some or

many of the leaf edges, effectively

increasing a basic resemblance)

(taking this language group as a

compiled noun or modular compound

conceptual object exposes a strategy
for identifying similar compiled noun
populations or more of the *leaf-storm-
feathers* neighborhood:)

a rain of softened fish bones

as if from deep within the blueprint
of a halibut

(where on a deep or cellular or
molecular level, iconic forms of
three-dimensional existences
seem essential to supporting
the forms that have grown, often
through aggregating, from iconic
form foundation; something that can
support the complexity by being the unit
that is repeated and mutated so as to
have the complexity)

a bone contract

**(once a contract is in place, once
group continues to interact in a self-
sustaining network, once there is
such** [temporary, on some scale]
**stability in a repeated-interaction
situation or event; once the gears are
turning, concern can be diverted to
areas less reliable**
[though the contract is not with
infallibility],
so a larger area of consideration

emerges, one that though
        further from a *leaf-storm-feather*
bone contract **direct impact,**
    ground-zero center,
    still encapsulates it from that
    distance, as any single atom
    in some part of a body
    may be a central point
    from which to navigate out to broader
    understandings)

a wide morning forms a sling

    (everything connected, part of, held
    together by, united by being part of
    existence, *sling* to emphasize the
temporary status of any conceptual
    coalition that forms meanings that
    can change through the regroupings
    reshufflings that characterize basic
    understandings of how what exists
    has contact with other things that exist;
    emphasizing consequences of
    movement, of existence being
    something in motion)

around the world

the morning wings it

    (existence itself is inexperienced
    at being existence when that word
    is used to suggest an uninterrupted

                    presence in progress since the
            beginning of any substance at all;
                    an assumption that this
                    all-encompassing existence is the first
                    and only; that if some other now
            inaccessible formats of presence
        was in place before the big bang, those
    previous formats and any that follow still
    form a single collective existence; so
                            the sling could have no experience to import
                            into this, the only and singular
                    existence, no matter how many
            universes emerge and perish, re-emerge
    somewhere and perish)

a prism shreds light

                            (greatest thing: sliced light of life,
                separation into components
                            even if such separation means
                destruction of integrity of the larger
                            structure in order to encounter
                            components on other scales)

into blazing garnish

                            (a feathering process dealing
                with perceiving light as its strands
                of visible and invisible spectra,
                understandings outside of what is
                observable via most unaided human
            perceptual systems, so is like a garnish,
                    is part of what can extend what is
            beautiful by linking to it, opening it,
                    locating counterparts and extensions.

Part of the garnish is the knowledge
placed on top what we think we know,
practical and aesthetic knowledge,
either or both of which could be placed
on the same thing under the garnish

that can modify
the perceptual function and value of the
garnish-enhanced plate, in this case
transforming *leaf*, visible spectrum, and
feathers into decorative fringe whose
basic pattern is linked to the essential
as are the molecules and atoms of the
fringe's underlying supportive structure;
aesthetic attributes are as much a part
of mind as what is considered objective
information)

fringe of burning shawl

(the visible spectrum as fringe,
the chromatic rainbow
as a form of light-shawl, the corona
defined during a solar eclipse,
anatomy of a crown on fire,
the God of Moses wrapped around
the shoulders, the genie out of the
bottle, the nuclear Shiva, beyond
the reach of death and toxins,
the burning shawl of malignancy to burn
the wearer being comforted in the
incredible power of such a shawl
hugging the life out of mortal shoulders;
a relinquishing of selfish selfhood to
belong to a generality of existence,
elemental substances that can become
anything, significance through events of

transformation, not the outcomes)

out of the west window, out of the east

                                      (a shawl that wraps and unwraps
                                 all continental shoulders and
                  hemispheres)

aerodynamic fire

                        (linked to movement of the jet stream
                    around the world, the changing
              distribution and configuration of
        shadows as light travels in and
    participates in patterns, some of which
                      depend of the earth moving in patterns
                    that interact with light and with light's
            sources)

the house is a rocket

                       (natural and synthetic forms of light,
              including fire, enter and exit human
          dwelling places, by controlled invitation,
      and also by other means, a house fire
                  suggestive of the fuel burn in the
          launching of spacecraft; a conversion
             that garnishes the house fire with
         humanity's searches for meaning
            throughout the universe)

the kitchen sink cockpit soars

                        (achievement, negative and positive)

Though air is displaced, there is immediate
atmospheric recovery

                        (air is torn through, but not torn up;
                        it re-knits as we walk through it, as we
            move objects)

—more impressive than flight is this
occupied model of forgiveness

                        (the re-knitting is linked to not keeping
                        a tally of what can be on a grudge to-do
            list)

A nest of splinters and embers

Shack soup

                        (though we rocket away, we explore
                        the largest scales of existence of which
            we are part; we do not rocket out of
        connections to ourselves, so we do not
      have to rocket away to study part of
    what is in space:
                        us, our world, our moon, our sun that
        touches us on earth, warms us well and
      too well now; though we soar and
    stretch and achieve, there is some
gravity in the situation,

and this aftermath of a house fire
is part of what the universe offers
—part of what we make, helped by the
universe, by what universes makes; we learn
this; we learn so much from so much
that we do not complete the task of
forming irrefutable understandings and
conclusions; we make shack soup, our
knowledge is as remnants, residue, as
flavoring, not necessarily the goose
which we might not have our hands on
at all yet, if ever. What does science do
with the realities of what can't be proven
[yet], yet science knows,

somehow, exists—an inability to prove
some core aspects of science's own
imagination; how humbling—and how
this urges continuation, tenacity,
longing,

curiosity—it's right here, can be felt,
can be intuited, our scraps of
information are part of something
important and yet)

the teacher's wings are two blackboards
strapped over his shoulders

(literally Kurdish teachers in Iran
taking schools to mountain
villages, portable learning spaces,
the intensity of the drive to know,
and to help others find ways to explore
what is knowable

within the parameters of the situations
in which they exist, the situations they
visit; learning can occur anywhere,
the most challenging situations are also
situations in which we construct ideas
about identity and purpose and
compensation;
but literally, as in the film *Blackboards*,
only one blackboard on a teacher's
back, but an opportunity for two wings
was irresistible and more likely to fly,
and can be imagined as easily as a
single blackboard on a back can be
imagined, since most who are most
likely to encounter the report would
probably have to imagine the
blackboard-backed teacher, having not
seen such teachers in person.
Then again, the imagination is
internally-based; sits with, and in, and
contains aspects of inspiration)

feathery lines of chalk

(even without magnification, though of
course also with it, the raggedness of a
chalk line is visible, the transfer of
chalkiness from chalk to hand is easy,
a generosity of shedding, of feathering;
each chalk flake can be magnified to
reveal structure, a feathered structure,
where the coastline or boundary is
irregular, looped, notched, and not
straight without defect and deviation

and diversion; there are numerous little
bifurcations, so many realities, each one
similarly feathered. We scratch the
surface; we make feathery bifurcating
marks on the surface that becomes
endless with bifurcations in the scratch.
There's no need to bother with depth as
the surface itself is inexhaustible.)

(in the endlessness: chances for forms
we can imagine better as we explore
less common, interactions and
intersections, a hypnotic or trance form
of prose poam a scratch on a tip of an
iceberg within a scratch)

say: this

is a wing

(a reference to movement of
blackboard-laden teachers, the flying of
knowledge,
curiosity is an aviator)

(curiosity navigates a scratch on a tip of
an iceberg within a scratch of
endlessness)

this is a wing

(it is an examination; the answer
is that experience is our wings;
we navigate and fly through meanings

and possibilities [including imagination],
the impact of what we encounter is part
of experience, impact translated into
facts of fantasy

and empirical facts
and facts of error
[that the prose poam is equipped to
[[adapt to]] handle];
just to say *it is snowing*
will be true somewhere
including the mindscape that can see
snow no matter where the physical body
is; so a literal snowfall, and the
aggregations of feathery landscapes
that emerge when the perfectly smooth
and straight are magnified; the snow
falls, some feathering occurs when the
scale of thinking opens its enhanced, its
extended eye)

when it snows, frozen
avian cloud masses swan the sky

cold strips their feathers

(plucks swans made of snow clouds
and drops the plucked snow feathers,
feather by feather, cell by cell)

from an altitude of ice age

spews tips of miniature Himalayas

(a scale shrink so that such promise
and possibility is a tool in your own

hand)

Hands cup what becomes liquid

                              (the story of transformation, of which
                    science is a part, of which everything is
                              a part, to be said to *exist* is a translation
                              of perceptual presence: we are, here
                    there are stories, empirical, invented,
            aesthetic stories of dreams of
understanding and understandings of
                    dreams)

                              (and after typing all this, I looked up
                              and saw a large grid of golden light on
                    my wall, a grid that covered the entirety
                              of what had been, till the grid arrived,
                              uncovered wall, a mural of sunset
                              [while tornadoes rage to the west in
                              Tazewell county] that wrapped the
                    interior of a corner, a radiant mural
                              not there at the outset of writing and
                    thinking my way through something
                              illuminating something in my own mind,
                              a mural that would not have been as
                    apparent had I not been so involved,
                    so located in the world of this idea
                    that was sufficiently bright to not require
                    me to seek the nearby lamps; the time
                    it would have taken to turn on external
lighting probably would have dimmed
                    the light kindled inside, but having
reached a spot where I could tell a story,
                    I looked up, maybe to see the story
better, to project it out of myself so that

it could reside with what inspired it,
and grabbed my camera phone to
capture the radiant mural that is gone
now, the grainy [feathered] two
megapixel image of the feathered edges
of light, even more textured by uneven,
feathered [when magnified] painted
plaster; that image the bones, the
remains of the mural, what survives
it, survival a translation of so much, of
everything with presence—so some of
Obama's audacity of hope and dreams,
his own radiant mural of biracial
presidency a reality he constructed for
himself in order to have something that
could be projected outside himself to
land on walls that really can be torn
down [I am so happy to be mixed, part
plaster, part feather, part golden grid,
golden ratio, mathematically divine]:
perfect, feathered bridge that is also
story of a bridge, the mixed prose poam
form reminds me of what is achievable
only through interactions and
intersections, a form that can be used
as a tool of investigation and
development)

A man dies praying

His hands cannot be pried apart

Roots and veins intertwine
and sew his hands

into eternal gratefulness

for this moment
(over which he has no power)

A tomato seed in his hands sprouts
(what luck that it's there)

so that

his heirloom heart
his hothouse brain

can ripen

(I wave to him, meet him halfway
on the feathered bridge between
miniature Himalayas, this prose poam
on the blackboard on my back
after it interacts with the heirloom heart
and hothouse brain
ripening on the blackboard on his back.)

This Did Not Happen

This did not happen

although I have memories of it:
a doctor unwrapping a tutu
so I knew I was in a hospital
but one unlike any other
practicing strange medicine
but this strangeness has been effective

A hospital for dancers?

I was in, pink,
sequined

I had been in a street,
an alley and

I was left there, tutu shredded,
I couldn't dance

anymore.

No animals other than myself, so the animal
in me

emerged

but tried to hurt no one

else.

Blue Coming

in response to Bob Holman's
"What You Can't Understand Is Poetry Is Connected to the Body Again"

Poetry is connected to the body,
part of my fingertips, just as blue as anything that ever was or will be blue—

—blue that dye aspires to, *true blue* denied to any sapphire,
    Logan Sapphire included, even
if she wears some on those blue fingers, blue spreads, consumes her
as if she hatched from an *Araucana* egg:

SHE IS BLUE, fingers, bluest hands ever, shoulders, breasts, every nook
    and cranny blue, big bad wolf says: *how blue you are!*
    The better to blue you....
She, so blue today, visits Offices of the *National Enquire*r to report
    on this surging of blue epidemic, Blue
    Bottle fly bluer than any sound buzzing, fly buzzing
    as blue as it can, making the Blues, making
The Blues mean something very different—such music from
    beating of wings, some of what has spread blue
    throughout her bluing, *dying* body,
blue buzz

even layers of atmosphere: *blue buzz*: name of a new *Crayola* crayon
    and marker, manufactured from her fingertips *Blue*
    Buzz Blood group. She bleeds an orgasmic paint set. She bleeds
    a blue layer her lover's face becoming blue (*dead blue/dead blew*)
    she's dreaming of again, blue as his face That defines blue for
    her blue orgasm, so much blue everywhere world become blue
    (*dead blue, dead blew*) for her—story of this massive bluing—
    true story on the cover of papers
—turning blue once in her atmosphere

Blue static Blue stuttering
Blue hands

Blue —*Code* Blue— coming together, what a mighty tincture —
    not exactly at the same time, but coming, connected to coming

Her fingertips writing a
Blue coming.

Me and Bubble Went to Memphis

Me and Bubble went to Memphis. I did everything I could for Bubble to have a better name, but that didn't happen.
Maybe because of how the name immediately stuck to the problematic motherhood of Bubble, how she wanted to burst
the bubble of her abdomen every step of the way, how she wanted to stick pins in Bubble's bubblehead, much too big for
the birth canal, bowling ball down twisted

alley, hair all slick   birth products, a dip in batter.
That was years ago. Way before   me and Bubble watched
the little rascals'   door-size cake, white
like every kitchen door   I've ever walked through
maybe I've entered only   test
kitchens, maybe there was some doubt   about everything being cooked
up when I entered the scene,   often dragging Bubble who
was compelled   since he couldn't be an astronaut
to wear a diving helmet   that he built himself, strict to specifications
in *Modern Mechanix*   so thrills
of lake bottoms   could be his, lust
for bubbling bogs,   he saw thick skinned
bubbles rising out of slime,   membranes
that housed feral embryos,   snake-mounds
of braid above the ear over a swell of head,   hairy hump graft
of miniature camel taking hold   in some maddening science
like the physics of going to Memphis   with Bubble, wearing a slab
of polyurethane-coated ribs,   pageant sash slabs
pageant sash slabs of ammunition.   He sprayed his mother's
face with polyurethane too, when he got there,   some of it

like bubbles of bacon
tiny globules of synthetic

breath of tiny bubbled tea, his
in depth of bog so thick
pushing his mother's casket
scouted good ones the four days
because of scouting, then once in
in diameter, thirteen inches deep, cookie
destined to be outfitted with plate
against his face, his lips
just as long as he didn't
the center of

splattering off the sides of her casket
grease, as if to coat particles of air,
sleet
going up the nose
air supply
he walked on it as he nearly drowned
turned botched kite off a cliff,
it took to get through Knoxville
Memphis, collecting tin cans ten inches
cans destined to become diving bells,
glass windows destined to be placed tight
pressed wider, nose flattened, the punch of the deep,
go too deep, just as long as he didn't get too near
anything, remaining in some margin, near some border, some sideline where he could have been unnoticed had it not
been for that collection of tin can diving bells, each one over a commandeered head like crude armor that he found out,
couldn't stop a bullet, repeat: couldn't stop a bullet, and Bubble couldn't stop firing, monogramming execution's polite
oversized hankies with airholes.

The Glory Prelude

This is the Glory Prelude
to a widow shrine system

I was raised to be forever convinced that Glory
was the prelude to everything

It worked

though I don't mean the same thing by Glory that my mother did, that my mother does.

Both of us acknowledge violence: God's mysterious prerogative for her
and for me: some atom smashing   convention-corrupting black holes
where bibles converge in a singularity with everything else:

a massive black hellhole

may be at the center of every galaxy

The household galaxy on Durkee where everyday she calls on Glory, her partner
since the death of my father in 1980:   a glory of bibles piled beside her
on my father's side of the bed

as weighted now as ever

King James version of him pressing into the pillow,
printed paper hair with red Jesus streak stains on satin

On our walks in the opposite direction of the Baptists and the Black Muslims,
my father and I stopped to look at every spider web full of windows
made by sticky framework
through which I saw a squeeze of Baby Flo's 800 pounds in a tent
that was her body's own revival, suspiciously like the tent my mother took me to
to be saved

without a carnival like this on the horizon

moved behind a veil-like framework
that used to cover faces at funerals

so that looking at grieving women, looking at my mother
was to see them, was to see her in a subdivided Baby Flo of confessionals
—what else am I to make of the framework of bars around her house

                                She has sealed herself in a widow shrine system
                                       of unchanging love for my father

                          the glory of which is the perfection of the seal, perfection of the ceiling

My father of wood, chandelier, and bibles continues
to be responsible for my mother to whom he is still connected

Roots of a tree he planted when I was born raise cement squares
of pregnant sidewalk

              His grave is a church, her god is my father's righteous proxy

in a neighborhood nothing like the glory that defined it when my father bought the house but as she puts it now, room after room of glory prelude, doors in and out of only

such prelude

to leave that house would break the connection, place her out of sync with the glory
she builds with the remnants of what she had and still has with daily rebuilding,

avoiding a lightness that could be hers as holes form
as it all turns to remnants.   Instead
it gains weight, means more, makes me remember every Saturday built
with *Spring* by Birdlegs and Pauline, *Forget About Me* by Prince Harold,
and *I Want to Thank You Pretty Baby* by Brook Benton

for the sound of glory days of my childhood
that had more than one glossy widow shrine note

If only I hadn't played for her *Amazing Grace* on my toy piano
when I was six and as proud as the day I got up and walked

even more impressively than Lazarus when he got up;
I had never walked before.

Sionon Epoch

1.

great word of honor

thy mother

with *Popeye's chicken*

delivered by wise persons

300 miles away, only ones

able to get exact *Popeye's* mama wants

> *love those biscuits!*
> *—like mama used to make*
>
> *in her dreams*

although extreme
insulin dependent diabetes, *hyper*-tension
thyroid

so out of control as if

she

no longer has one

poor baby poor baby no matter
how old one becomes still
somebody's baby

> (though no longer a dream
> *baby*)

Dreams have not stopped, but
no longer baby dreams—these dreams

have matured

as Popeye Doyle detectives, break

dream rules,

whatever's necessary
to catch drug smugglers

drunken Popeye's chicken
tastes even better

and even fights God, a Cerullo

god

somehow better than any other

god
        cabinets of medicine

discarded, useless
prescriptions, a real God

doesn't need them

yet everyone, dreaming or who
stops relying on power of medicine

to heal and stave off
effects of

aneurysms and much worse

die

some same night that Amy Winehouse
goes back to black

babies, no one admits
to dreaming of them,

no

one, two, three
cans of spinach each bicep
clothed

in a right mind, a dream
mind

better

sí

crack split

my dream sky,
my head, dream skull
full of dreams, overflowing
brain spinach of aneurysm
strong to the finish
of the dream

a jellyfish affair

mothered

2.

even in
the *Lake of Fire* she used to work
in Marine Towers West,

Gold Coast

by Lake Erie, great lake
greater when it burns

in a dream all grown up right

in the church, tiny storefront church
where ordination papers

signed by Cerullo himself
are kept—no finer
diploma on earth

which doesn't interest her

No

losing touch until

Jesus

laid her down
diabetic coma

poor baby, poor baby,

divorce

isn't dry

only man

to dream about, care about think about

is Jesus, dream man Jesus, three days

in the tomb of impossible
dreams, even the dream

of dying someday, wet feet
and all, cans of spinach
in the storefront dried with
Towels from old boxes of *Breeze*
detergent

laid down
by none else than Jesus
look out

for wolves,
the taste they have for

succulent little lambs
so willing

to lay down at dream feet
that can walk on the lake of fire

that burns even better when it's cold, as
crystals form

a dream of my hand, heel as pure
crystals
dream crystal
crystallizing
61 crystals

so far

candles on a cake

my frozen feet seem to have flakes
from Popeye's

fried chicken all over them,
roughest skin
on my body
—no one dreams of that;
not *dream*-worthy skin at all
geometries of these crystals,
each a stegosaurus plate

—no

sí o no?

Sionon
story of a dream kitchen
with *stegosaurus plates fine china*

—always yes to that, Popeyes
on the side

burning, burning, burning
up
and burning down

perfect, perfect burning. . . .
wisdom God gave me in
a dream of giving me wisdom

wise enough
to only dream only that

while *Jesus laid her dow*n
with wolves in *Lake of Fire Amusement Park,*

3.

Little Pigs
house of straw, dream house of sticks

bad dreams?
sí

Little Pig, Little Pig, a trinity of us, you know
what that means, Jesus will

lay you down right at my feet,
I just need something to eat
fun times all
Let me in,
not by the *hair of my chinny chin chin*

I'll huff and I'll puff then
better than any vacuum
cleaner, till those houses come down
wolf is still a windbag dream *(coming true)*
when he goes to the third Pig's dream house
of bricks

wasted, completely wasted
huffing and puffing climbs
down the chimney, invents
a form of Santa, Wolf
in red suit from embers
scraping

his *Frank Lucas-style* fur coat

that he doesn't have to remove
to enter cauldron of boiling water

lid on until
Big Bad soup is ready
as a dream can ever be

Aneurysm of Firmament

Piñata sky broken, ruptured!

—what stick hit it?
    —what cosmic event cracked it open?

(—good thing it did!—)

—comets and more

rain of treats

        light itself showers down

                        BRIGHT
                                                belts

                        ropes

a boxing match

light swirls into poles & other delights

                —such RUPTURE

                                        my brain the sun

in the solar system I am
                RUPTURED!

                                        solar flares
                                        solar winds

& even more!—coronal mass ejection—massive bursts!
                the sun becomes a red giant—solar maxima!
& I direct traffic!—plenty of Nissans!—red hot off assembly lines
                from the center of Botticelli's painting
                the birth of brown Venus, sheer sparkling gauze over me

as *Gallifrey* burns
                    Buckwheat's hair on fire
                    —fountains of luminous combustion!
13 Doctors heal
                    this blazing epidemic
                                  each regeneration of the Doctor has him
produce spiky burning arms
                    fountains of illuminated spikes
                                  each a protrusion from the head

                          of a hijacked Cameroonian stink ant!

sparklers   pinwheels

kaboom, kaboom, kaboom

more
and
more
Daleks
fall

                                        no rupture, and no light!

something has to break!

Part 3

comets have to fall, and fall hard, into *Midnight Sun,* 1961
Twilight Zone

—*optical illusion dimensions*—sun enlarges and enlarges

imminent end of Earth.

At last. . . Poor Norma. . . Last one in apartment building
—blood is boiling—*rupture* is about to happen—I will bleed again, a crazed menstrual cycle
(*Norma was dreaming, sick and feverish—escaped the chill really going on*
—either way, Earth in atypical orbit):

—post-menopausal now, so this blood comes from my head:

this is the way the world ends

all condemned by existence

                         lightning illuminating those veins in the ceiling that is firmament
Gallifrey all

lightning; seems to exist only when there's *hocus pocus of fire*

. . . but this time*, Gallifrey* saved, by Time Lords, who? Doctors, that's who! all combining
their strength into streaks of light *life-preservers in*

deep freeze

on Gallifrey, Gallifrey home!—there is no other!—light of battle erupts!—in these multiple skies!—
planet surrounded by radiant ra-di-a-tion belts!—the brain that this salvation is breaks—writing is on
the wall—that none of them want:

NO MORE! NO MORE!

left with guilt of responsibility of billions of deaths

Gallifrey protected by ice
                                       cold
but just as brilliant, scintillates away and away and away

The most splendid rupture ever! Bring on rupturing aneurysms!—changed my life, just as they should!

Shake up this firmament! -shake it to the east, shake it to the west, shake it to the one you love the best and risk

being
Frozen

with Gallifrey is also hope! that sparkles down transfigured
in tea cups. . . a sweet prescription, full of inspiration, hope of inspiration's
inspired healing!—sweetened by rays of light, spikes of rapturous (freebie) aneurysm, bulging veins,
like thermometer bulbs about to pop:

healing-cure-healing-cure-healing-cure-healing-cure-healing-cure-healing-cure:
                                        :goes the weasel,
Hello again, Norma: weasel in a welcome to Midnight Sun salvation:

my aneurysms, one repaired, and the other: ready to blow

                              sky high

(part 3a)

Poor Amy

broke, ruptured 23 July 2011—*cracked*
same day one of my own cranial aneurysms ruptured, broke in (that burglar)
my head . . . repaired!—I have beautiful scars, staple holes, unintentional scarification; hair
grown wild around them, cleats

were

stationed there (with)

one more aneurysm: timebomb! *ticktock ticktock, ticktock hickory dickory dock:*
Hickory, dickory, dock.
The mouse ran up the clock.
The clock struck one gleaming, glistening aneurysm

rhythms of light;
and then there was, you know

how it is, how it's always been, how
it will be

the brilliant repetition

sky high

Gallifrey falls no more

Wannabe Hoochie Mama Gallery of Realities' Red Dress Code

I have learned to be still
I have learned that I don't have to go anywhere
to find the center of the universe
Anything can be that center

From any point, any squiggle, any speck of dust,
I can widen
what that speck, what that squiggle includes
what that speck is willing
to embrace
what that speck and squiggle can be the center of
until everything that is possible to get to
is included in the circle

so I have learned to be still
to let everything pass through me
a sieve
a net
that manages to catch
awareness of what passes through

And as things pass through me,
I also pass through them

in an exchange of tiny ropes of essences
(so I can wear necklaces anywhere)
My DNA is a necklace

There's a claiming by me
of some of what passes through
and what passes through me claims some
of the parts of me passed through

so these point by point, squiggle by squiggle
touches and embraces—*these beautiful exchanges!*—
together make up realities

and can be put together in any order
to form one big remarkable thing
as what passes through me
passes through what passes through
everything else
in every form of reality
that is possible to make
from any locations possible
in any reality that is possible

This happens

including realities
made in imagination
for so much passes through
the mind
—*O see, O hear, O touch, O taste, O feel*
how things connect—
Because of what's possible
Because of all the hands
all the specks—which can be any shape
made of any substance
which can be any form—
Because of all the hands
all the specks in the touching in the exchanges
in feeling and groping their way
Because of all the hands involved
in pieces in the shufflings of pieces
of maybe unlimited numbers
of flexible realities

& because of how easy it is to connect dots
one day red might arrive
some planes and geometries might meet
an event of red dress might happen
for dress is not always red
red happens to dress
and dress sometimes happens to red
red dress is an event

red might slip by dress
when they are on paths that do not cross
somewhere for some length of time
Dress might elude red
in a pursuit red might be reluctant to abandon

I do not put on a red dress
It is something outside of wardrobes
acceptable for me
some of what I do
some of what I believe and practice
could be questioned
if I put on a red dress
but if I am still
an event of red dress might happen
if I do not move from this spot
so that specks and squiggles of both red
and dress
can find me
then there will be
—while they pass through—
realities I can feel
specks of red
and specks of dress
passing through different
parts of me at different speeds
for different lengths of time

during which hoochie mama gets in
at least one of all possible equations

and I will walk out of here
where I have stood as if hard at work
on display in a gallery
no worse for the where I've been

apparently unchanged

but the red dress
was put on under my skin
and it fits me
there

O it's so amazing
that everything that passes through
fits.

Higginson Matters in "Magnificent Culture of Myopia"

(a poem of singularities—for Keith)

In Chicago, we look out *Mandarin Moon*
highest windows, and I see distortions,
nightmares, as my-opia prevails, resurfaces as
it surfaced in trigonometry; it was

the first time I swore
there was no such thing as *parabola*,
no such thing as *abscissa*:

I never saw them
as I never see what Higginson looks like
up close in *perfect* detail, every problem
solved, every wrinkle
removed, all of him chalk

in Mr. Ansari's hand
magnificent sixth finger, whiter than
his profession, his lab coat with *mathematician*
stitched in a roller coaster, an harmonics
of loud letters on his back; even his eyes,
—not Higginson blue—failures

were written on, red subscripts, rocks
and infinitesimal exponents surrounding
centers dark with explosions of visions
of what could be found only in numbers:
Higginson: the integer, one, home
coming singularity Higginson: constant, primary
ordinate, coordinate of my-opia: all mine

while Ansari wrote invisibly
on the board, his hand moving along
black expanse and along my own back, Higginson
writes a wave from a *dream* baby ocean
he blesses, caresses, casts spells

this substitute teacher, this Higginson integer
of unity: one, his own cube: one, his own square: one
against his singularity tests: his name Ahmed Said

meaning God's gift to women:
Higginson the only *unity*
integer beside me

Although he's available
for conferences in bed, I never see
clearly what he wants, can see only
Higginson one singularity of infinite coastline
that doesn't resolve until I get my glasses
his corrections are too familiar with my face
in the face of Higginson's blue-eyed exams that
brush my mouth as if to blot
excess lip gloss *not that there ever can be too much*
Higginson in a new math cycle
from my back row desk

where birds sang me answers through
glass, Higginson's chest is written on with reflection
of him—*all algebraic better*—than the board
was written on, he looked as unreal
as irrational numbers and absurd roots,
my very mind affected and infected
with swarms of Higginson integers he introduces
on a *Higginson-Ansari merger, unity-form of Einstein-Rosen*
purely mathematical wormhole bridge

in singularity lessons I thought were about chromosomes
and sexist destiny: everything plotted
on x and y axes,
some of them negative numbers,
some of them able to cancel out the others,
solutions of zero or 1—without exception

except that Higginson brings with him a
whole new set of rules and insists
nothing is absolute
and constantly shifts values
little love triangle: *Higginson-Ansari and me*

same year that I get close to Higginson,
to survey, triangulate his body, locate three
dimensional points of his position in my life, on that bridge,
I scan his mouth so that I can find even in the dark
beacons in his lips that help me navigate to him and find
best angles of an infinite kiss that solve something
meant to be nebulous

during those hours that I can't find him, when
he's as shadowy as faith, his edges as unsure
yet in that uncertainty, his lips become soft,
blurred, compassionate, betraying the fraying
that betrays good use: a fog in rags
as he tears my *xs* clothes off me
so many encompassing angles in a somewhat
silvery number line follies of stationary
missionary position

without my glasses
best not to wear them to bed although I do to see
Higginson better, one singularity beside me,
his back as creamy as the milky way should be,
those angles from where he is to the heaven where it is, those
triangles that appear when I look at stars through
the telescope of his arms and see
that hazed perimeter, a fuzziness partial arch-ing arc-ing truth

of the fuzzy logic of re-growing hair in the middle of the night
entire hotel alive with a growing fuzziness about to cover

all Chicago in his mouth, every equation
that doesn't add up to our being here together
until the numbers are fudged, and they are pliable indeed
in the fuzziness of these uniting moments that

bring us closer and closer together until we become
beneficiaries of each other and the peach of a moment like this,
heirs of fuzz, scant fur of beginner mold about to bless
bread with blue beard—and we're about wearing such fuzzy,
such nebulous raiment—in fact, I'm named

for this slightly less than magnificent effect
—even rocks put on moss suggesting that anything
can become Higginson sweet, Higginson ripe, Higginson good
for me softly loving me in these memories as distant as
that peach of a moon growing sweeter,
with a worm-hole in deeper craters
with distance, so sweet
I taste (thinking of him and where love given a chance to grow
might lead—*without family, jobs, grief, any other responsibilities, distractions of nightmares*
turning back the clock again and again to younger)
peaches from an Eden triangulated from the survey of all
cooperating equipment of measurement, just soft enough, gentle
enough to be that hoped for and prayed for mirage
and every fata morgana: *journey's end*

—*I don't have to look for this again:* it's right
(angled) and right (beside me) as a lens
falls out of my glasses so the left eye strains
against clarity, as if a screen has been pulled down
locking my left eye in a neuritis of what could be permanent
sinister my-opia myopia

the other eye, the one always right refused
to let things merge in blur the way they will have to

if brightness comes with a glare that can seem angelic
if seeing is believing as that glare provides light with
halos of circular wings; blur and no distinction,
no endings or beginnings, just that escape

that Higginson now is, mathematical escape, it all
adds up to his one; all multiplies by one peach, one delectable
furry ball, celestial game of pool: *Earth pocket*, nothing else
I see standing so close beside him is able to find a way
to sustain life as it escapes from focus, all lines crooked,
crinkled, wobbling and now as if we're even older
with unsteady gait and hands experiencing such *shaking* when
we're this close, barely a
fuzzy ball of a peach between us, two of them on my chest,
fuzziness magnified, not there otherwise Higginson experiencing

such *shaking* when he tries to grasp one of those peaches
and realizes this peach is more powerful than we are
          peach, sweet orb
drupe of drupes dangling from a branch that is *Earth*
peachy as can be
dangling in a galactic arm playing *peach ball*

with all the spheres, rotating them
all at once: peach of my own body, at first, extended
into the whole Higginson universe, *peach of me* alive
in his fuzzy mouth, dark as the wandering night sky, more
powerful than we are *simple little peach*, as fuzzy as can be
—*o how we Methuselahs shake*
from its magnetism steadily drawing me close to him and redrawing
boundaries of this *peachy-keen* existence

when he finally lifts it electrified to his mouth,
its fuzz much more incredible than the start of puberty,

little squiggles of fuzz, little hairs magnified into roadways
ablaze with population and suggestions that it might still
be possible to invent a peach of lamb when this means everything
we are not and can't be once we open the door
and break the spell of the world being dressed
as a simple peach: softly, softly, even the weapons
appear softly, reveal their leniency
to magnificent myopia, softly

lunatics respond, softly is therapy
myopically beginning—perhaps it will last,
perhaps visual details softly dispersed
into static will hold, won't be repaired:
a big peach seen from afar is on my screen
and Higginson watches it carefully

when the cable's out	dot matrices peach
when the cable's out	I can appreciate Higginson molecules
watching the static	I am grateful for Higginson atoms that he
watching the static	releases into the peach on my chest

I can feel the fuzz under the screen, touch the static, hear it
on the radio once out of clarity's range of belief
in comprehension—humble blur,
we are indeed admirers of this blossoming empire
of peached existence between us, for it is penitence
I see without my glasses

which Higginson removes
and puts on the nightstand

NOTES

Many of the new poems in this volume are transcriptions of video POAMS [products of acts of making], which can be found on the author's Forkergirl YouTube channel, and in installations around the country at such venues as the Pulitzer Arts Foundation in St. Louis, Missouri, and the Work Gallery in Ann Arbor, Michigan. Scores for many of the POAMS were composed by Ansted Moss, the author's son.

"This Did Not Happen" reflects how the author perceived the world shortly after surviving, miraculously, the rupture of a cranial aneurysm.

"Blue Coming" is a response to "What You Can't Understand Is Poetry Is Connected to the Body Again" by Bob Holman.

"Sionon Epoch" is a collaborative, limited fork POAM, written by the author and a friend, Higginson. It includes references to *Doctor Who*, the sci-fi television series.

"Higginson Matters in the Magnificent Culture of Myopia" is a salvaging and revision of a poem, "The Magnificent Culture of Myopia," which appeared in *Tokyo Butter* (Persea, 2006).

ABOUT THE AUTHOR

THYLIAS MOSS (née Brasier) was born in 1954, in Cleveland, Ohio, to a multiracial (African American, Native American, Indian, Caucasian) father and an African American mother. After teaching at Phillips Academy in Andover, Massachusetts, she taught for many years at the University of Michigan, where she is now Professor Emerita in the Department of English and the College of Art & Design.

Moss is the author of the poetry collections *Tokyo Butter* (2006), *Slave Moth* (2004), *Last Chance for the Tarzan Holler* (1999, finalist for the National Book Critics Circle Award), *Small Congregations: New and Selected Poems* (1993), *Rainbow Remnants in Rock Bottom Ghetto Sky* (1991), *At Redbones* (1990), *Pyramid of Bone* (1989), and *Hosiery Seams on a Bowlegged Woman* (1983). She has also published a memoir, *Tale of a Sky-Blue Dress*, and a children's book, *I Want to Be*. For her poetry, she has received numerous honors, including the Witter Bynner Prize and fellowships from the National Endowment for the Arts, the Guggenheim Foundation, and the MacArthur Foundation.

Moss is founder of Limited Fork Poetics, an interdisciplinary creative and theoretical process combining elements of film, sound, poetry, computer science, and other disciplines. She lives in Ypsilanti, Michigan.